A Caretaker of Love

Standing staring at Neula was the most elegant, the most handsome man she had ever seen.

In a nervous voice she asked:

"Who are . . . you?"

"I think that is the question I should be asking you!" the Marquis replied as he walked towards her. "I understood that my house was empty!"

"*Your* house?" Neula gasped. "Then you are the . . . Marquis of Kerne!"

"I am! And now perhaps you will explain who you are!"

For a moment Neula was so bemused that she almost told the truth. Then she said with difficulty:

"I . . . I am Neula . . . Borne . . . one of your . . . new caretakers!"

A Camfield Novel of Love
by Barbara Cartland

"*Barbara Cartland's novels are all distinguished by their intelligence, good sense, and good nature . . .*"

— ROMANTIC TIMES

"*Who could give better advice on how to keep your romance going strong than the world's most famous romance novelist, Barbara Cartland?*"

— THE STAR

Camfield Place,
Hatfield
Hertfordshire,
England

Dearest Reader,

Camfield Novels of Love mark a very exciting era of my books with Jove. They have already published nearly two hundred of my titles since they became my first publisher in America, and now all my original paperback romances in the future will be published exclusively by them.

As you already know, Camfield Place in Hertfordshire is my home, which originally existed in 1275, but was rebuilt in 1867 by the grandfather of Beatrix Potter.

It was here in this lovely house, with the best view in the county, that she wrote *The Tale of Peter Rabbit*. Mr. McGregor's garden is exactly as she described it. The door in the wall that the fat little rabbit could not squeeze underneath and the goldfish pool where the white cat sat twitching its tail are still there.

I had Camfield Place blessed when I came here in 1950 and was so happy with my husband until he died, and now with my children and grandchildren, that I know the atmosphere is filled with love and we have all been very lucky.

It is easy here to write of love and I know you will enjoy the Camfield Novels of Love. Their plots are definitely exciting and the covers very romantic. They come to you, like all my books, with love.

Bless you,

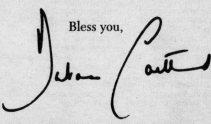

CAMFIELD NOVELS OF LOVE
by Barbara Cartland

Other books by Barbara Cartland

A NEW CAMFIELD NOVEL OF LOVE BY

BARBARA CARTLAND

A Caretaker of Love

JOVE BOOKS, NEW YORK

A CARETAKER OF LOVE

A Jove Book/published by arrangement with
the author

PRINTING HISTORY
Jove edition/February 1988

ISBN: 0-515-09442-0

Jove Books are published by the Berkley Publishing Group,
200 Madison Avenue, New York, New York 10016.
The name "JOVE" and the "J" logo
are trademarks belonging to Jove Publications, Inc.

PRINTED IN THE UNITED STATES OF AMERICA

10 9 8 7 6 5 4 3 2 1

AUTHOR'S NOTE

When William IV came to the throne, the Court changed drastically. After the gaiety, the extravagance, and the licence of George IV, it was hard for many of the aristocratic Bucks and Beaux to adjust themselves to the new regime.

The King concentrated on economies, the Queen on morality—the Royal yachts were cut down from five to two and the Stud reduced to half its former size; a hundred and fifty exotic birds which had delighted George IV were presented to the Zoological Society.

The Court was dull and dowdy, the Princess Lieven, the witty, sharp-tongued wife of the Russian Ambassador wrote:

> *You know full well what life is like at*
> *Court—Dinners of forty people who are not*
> *all of them remarkably interesting; and no*
> *possibility of having any reasonable*
> *conversation. In the evening we all sit at the*

round table—the King snoozes, the Queen does needlework.

Greville, who dined at Windsor during Royal Ascot Races, wrote:

> *What a* changement de decoration. *No longer George IV, capricious, and misanthropic, liking nothing but the society of listeners and flatterers . . . but a plain, vulgar, hospitable gentleman . . . with a frightful Queen and a posse of bastards, a Whig Minister, no foreigners, and no Toad-eaters at all.*

chapter one

1832

Neula heard her mother scream and put her hands up to her ears.

Never had she imagined she would be so appalled and shocked as she was when she returned from Florence, where she had been at School.

When Charles Sherborne, her dashing, irresistible father, died, her small but happy world had come to an end.

It was inevitable that he would sooner or later have an accident riding the wild, unbroken horses, which were all he could afford.

Yet he rode with the dashing brilliance with which he did everything else.

It was also inevitable that, when he was no longer with them, his wife and his only daughter should discover that he had left a mountain of debts.

He had enjoyed life with a zest that was infectious, and

he had never troubled himself, or anyone else, with what was unpleasant.

But Louise Sherborne had looked with dismay and apprehension at the multitude of bills which she had found hidden away in her husband's writing-desk.

Irrepressible, never facing up to anything unpleasant when bills arrived, he had merely shut them away in a drawer and conveniently forgotten about them.

"What shall we do?" Mrs. Sherborne asked pitiably.

The daughter of an irascible but distinguished soldier, General Sir Alexander Tremaine, her father, had cut her off with the proverbial shilling.

It was not surprising when against his wishes and his advice she had run away with the Honourable Charles Sherborne.

The General was well aware that he had not a "penny to bless himself with."

His father, Lord Borne, lived frugally in a house that was falling about his ears.

He was unable to play any part in the County because he could not afford it.

Because his son Charles was so handsome and so popular, he naturally expected him to make a good marriage.

There were, Lord Borne knew, several heiresses he was continually meeting in London.

Sir Alexander had had the same aspirations for his daughter.

'She is as pretty,' he thought, 'as her mother was when I married her and growing prettier year by year.'

It was a shock to both sets of parents when they learnt that Charles and Louise had run away to get married.

They were so blissfully happy that nothing their parents could say would have evoked any response.

Charles had never listened to his father's admonishing

him to "marry money," and Louise would have been inhuman if she had resisted him.

They were each consumed with a passion for the other.

It was as true as the love of Romeo and Juliet, of Dante and Beatrice, and that sung by the Troubadours.

It was also apparent to everybody who came in touch with them.

The exception, of course, being the General and Lord Borne.

"How could I live without you, my darling?" Charles asked.

He looked so irresistibly handsome as he spoke that Louise could only melt into his arms.

She forgot that she had no money for the housekeeping or to pay a servant to wait on them.

Charles had an allowance of one hundred pounds a year from his grandmother, who was beguiled by him, as every other woman was, whatever her age.

Unfortunately, however, she had not settled any money on him before she died.

Two weeks before Charles was killed, he and Louise were faced once again with the problem of how they could make ends meet.

He was making a little money by breaking in horses, which he sold at a profit.

Since he had to go to London to find a buyer, and look smart while he did so, the profit, when it did come, was a small one.

What his grandmother had done, however, was to pay in advance for Neula's education in Florence.

"You and Louise may have found the world well lost for love," she said to her grandson, "but Neula is going to be very lovely when she grows up."

She smiled at him and then went on:

"She should have the opportunity of shining in the Social World that was yours until you threw it away."

"I gave it up for something very much more important than money and social success," her grandson had replied rather truculently. "It is a rare condition called 'Happiness'!"

His grandmother laughed.

"That is true, but you cannot expect Neula to be content with watching you and her mother mooning about romantically in a dead-and-alive village!"

She stopped speaking a moment and then added:

"The only men she is likely to meet are the Vicar or the Grocer!"

Charles had laughed and said:

"We are very grateful for your concern, Grandmama, and I hope it is as practical as your words."

"It is," his grandmother replied. "As soon as Neula is sixteen, she is going to Florence for two years to what I hear is the best and most-up-to-date Academy for Young Ladies in the whole of Europe."

Louise had been more grateful than Charles, who had disliked the idea of losing his daughter.

But as his grandmother had put down the money to pay for her fees before she died, Neula knew that her future for the next two years was assured.

At the same time, she did not wish to leave her mother alone and unprotected.

"I shall not go!" she decided after her father's death.

Louise had hugged her.

"Of course you must, dearest! It is the opportunity of a lifetime, and I shall be quite all right here."

"With no money and all those debts?" Neula asked harshly. "Darling Mama, you have to eat!"

4

Then almost, it seemed at the time, in answer to their prayers, Sir Horace Harlow appeared.

He was a man over fifty who had bought several horses from Charles Sherborne.

He turned up a few days after the Funeral to see if there were any animals left which might interest him.

Neula secretly thought he was hoping to get some "on the cheap."

But when he had talked to her mother, Neula having tactfully left them alone, he had paid considerably more than they were worth.

What was more, he called the next day to arrange for them to be collected, and again the day after that to make sure there was no mistake about his instructions.

By the end of the week he had asked Louise Sherborne to marry him.

For a moment Louise had stared at him in sheer bewilderment, finding it difficult to understand what he was saying.

"I know you are very unhappy at losing your husband," he said, "and I know you do not love me."

He paused a moment and then continued:

"But I will teach you to love me, and, as I am a very rich man, I can give you everything that you need, and will, of course, look after Neula as well."

It was these words which made Mrs. Sherborne consider him seriously.

She was well aware that although Neula's School fees were paid, they would have to find money for her journey to Florence.

She would also need clothes.

They had to be better made and more expensive than what she had worn while helping her father with the horses and her mother in the house.

Every nerve in Louise's body screamed that after loving Charles, she would die rather than be the wife of another man.

Yet she knew that it would be intolerably selfish to have Neula poverty-stricken at home once she had finished her education.

All the Tremaine relations had ignored Louise when she had run away with Charles, with the exception of her brother Hugh.

A few years younger than his sister, he was a wild, irresponsible young man, who had spent an astronomical sum of money enjoying himself in London.

In consequence, Louise heard he was largely to blame for the General's death, which had happened only a few months before.

He had, in fact, had a stroke when he found out how much his son owed.

On his death practically everything he left had gone to paying Hugh's bills.

Not content with this, Hugh had, during a night of debauchery and gambling, lost Tremaine Park, which he had inherited from his father, on the turn of a card.

When she learned of this first through the newspapers, then through the Vicar of the village in which Tremaine Park stood, Louise Sherborne had cried despairingly.

For the first time since her marriage she realised that she still loved her home, and the things in it which had belonged to her mother.

Although she had never been able to go back, she knew now that it was where she belonged.

She was like a child who was suddenly orphaned, as she actually was.

Only Charles's arms around her and his lips on hers had been able to comfort her.

There was worse to come, for two months later Hugh Tremaine was engaged in a duel in Green Park and shot dead the man he was fighting.

To save being arrested, he crossed the Channel and enjoyed himself in Paris until, having been wounded in yet another duel, he died of his injuries.

Louise was aware that her brother was dead only when she was written to by the solicitors who were administering his affairs.

It did not surprise her to hear that he, too, had left large debts which were unlikely ever to be cleared.

There were, therefore, no close relations who could look after Neula.

Louise also knew that distant cousins would not be particularly interested in the daughter of a woman who had done something so reprehensible as to elope with a penniless young man.

Therefore, after much heart-searching and spending nights on her knees in prayer, she finally accepted Sir Horace Harlow.

Because she was in deep mourning, she and Sir Horace were married very quietly at a Registry Office in London.

They went for their honeymoon to a house he owned at Newmarket, where no one was likely to notice them at that time of the year.

Neula was sent to Sir Horace's large and rather ugly house in Oxfordshire.

Before she left he told her genially to buy what clothes she required before she left for Florence.

She found there were some good dressmakers in Oxford, and there was a seamstress employed in the house who could alter anything she bought.

She could also make her the more simple gowns she would require at School.

7

Neula was intelligent enough to realise that it was a very fashionable Academy.

As the pupils came from some of the most distinguished families in Italy and France, they would certainly be well-dressed.

She was sure, moreover, that the French girls would have a *chic* that was almost impossible to find in England.

At sixteen Neula already had a good figure and was also exceedingly attractive with her fair hair touched with red.

The colour resembled her father's while her huge green eyes flecked with gold she had inherited from her mother.

When her mother and stepfather joined her at the Towers after their honeymoon, she was aware that her mother looked pale.

Although she was careful not to speak of it, she was obviously unhappy.

Neula attributed this to the fact that her mother was still desperately miserable at losing her adored husband.

Neula could not, however, help appreciating that Sir Horace was being extremely generous.

He bought her mother clothes that came from the most fashionable dressmakers in Bond Street.

The jewels which glittered round her neck and on her wrists were, Neula guessed, worth a small fortune.

When Neula left for Florence, she was thinking that if nothing else, her mother would live in a luxury she had never known since she had run away from home.

There was an army of servants to wait on her at The Towers, and it was obvious that Sir Horace was infatuated with his new wife.

Having been a widower for fifteen years, he found her companionship something he had missed even more than he realized.

"Take care of yourself, my dearest!" Louise had said to her daughter when she left.

"And Sir Horace will take care of you, Mama!" Neula had replied.

"I hope . . . so," her mother had said a little doubtfully.

"I could never have left you alone with no money and nothing to do, and you would have missed Papa unbearably if I had not been there to cheer you up."

"I miss him . . . now!" Louise had said with a little sob in her voice.

The words were spoken in a whisper.

Then she looked over her shoulder as if she were afraid they might be overheard.

Neula arrived in Florence with a generous allowance of pocket-money from Sir Horace.

Her wardrobe of clothes, to her satisfaction, compared well with the gowns worn by the other pupils.

Because she was intelligent, she applied herself diligently to learning everything that was possible.

She made friends with girls of different nationalities so that she could learn to speak their languages.

After her first year she carried off a number of prizes which she was sure would delight her mother.

She wrote home twice a week and Louise wrote her long, loving letters telling her what they were doing.

She described the parties they attended as soon as she was in half-mourning, and the Race-Meetings where Sir Horace watched his horses win many prizes.

Neula was very perceptive, and sensitive to those she loved.

She was aware without her mother writing it down that she regretted that her first husband could not have had the same fine horses to ride and to race as Sir Horace had.

In fact, Neula realized as she recalled the contents of the letters, her mother had very seldom mentioned him.

When she arrived home it was to find that things were very different from what she had anticipated.

She had not been inside the front door of The Towers for an hour before she realized that Sir Horace had become very strange in the two years she had been away.

He looked much older and his hair was almost white, but it was not his looks which perturbed her so much as his behaviour.

When she left for Florence he had been fawning on her mother.

He complimented her, made it very clear how much he adored her, and found nothing too expensive or too trivial if it would make her happy.

Now he was a different man altogether.

He contradicted everything his wife said, and was unaccountably and continually rude to her.

The way he spoke and looked at her made Neula think that he actively disliked her.

When they were alone, Neula said as she put her arms around her mother's shoulders:

"What has happened, Mama? Why is Sir Horace so disagreeable?"

Tears filled her mother's eyes, and at first she said:

"I . . . I do not want to . . . talk about it."

"But you cannot leave me in ignorance, Mama!" Neula protested. "I was thinking while I was in Florence that you would be happy because Sir Horace was so kind."

She paused and then went on:

"But now he is extremely rude to you at luncheon-time and everything you said seemed to annoy him."

"I know . . . I know!" Louise said miserably. "I cannot

. . . help it! I have tried and tried . . . but there is . . . nothing I can . . . do!"

"I do not understand," Neula said.

She knew her mother was debating whether to prevaricate or tell her the truth.

Then as if it were a relief to have somebody to share her troubles with, she said in a voice that her daughter could hardly hear:

"When he married me . . . Sir Horace thought I would give . . . him . . . an heir. His first wife had been unable to do so, and he . . . thought as I was still young enough . . . there would be no . . . difficulty."

Neula drew in her breath.

This was something she had not expected.

"It is not . . . my fault," her mother went on. "I promise you it is not! It is Horace who is not . . . capable of having any . . . children, but he . . . blames me!"

"Surely somebody should tell him what is wrong?" Neula suggested.

"The doctor who is a kind man has . . . tried but he will not . . . listen," her mother murmured. "He has made up his mind that I should give him a son."

She gave a deep sigh and then went on:

"Because one has not . . . materialised, he hates me, and wishes . . . I were dead!"

Neula gave a little cry of horror.

"I cannot believe it, Mama! I am sure you should not say such things!"

Then she realised that her mother was crying and she held her close and kissed her cheek.

"It is all right, Mama," she said. "I am home and I will look after you."

"No, darling, you must not interfere," her mother said. "It was a . . . mistake for me to . . . marry him, but I was

. . . thinking of you . . . and now there is . . . nothing I can do . . . nothing."

Her voice was choked with tears.

When Neula left her she sat in her own large and luxurious bedroom wondering what she could do to help her mother in what seemed an impossible situation.

Twenty-four hours later she was to realise that it was far more serious than she thought.

Because she wanted her daughter near her, Lady Harlow had put Neula in the room which was next to her own, while on the other side was her *Boudoir*.

Beyond that was Sir Horace's room, the Master Bedroom.

The first night of Neula's return they had an extremely uncomfortable dinner, when Sir Horace had been even ruder to her mother than he had been at luncheon.

When they went to bed she felt as if she had stepped into a nightmare from which she must awake.

She undressed, but instead of getting into bed she thought she would go to her mother, to see if she could talk to her.

Perhaps, although it seemed impossible, she might find a solution to her problems.

Neula had thought innocently, after what her mother had told her, that she and her stepfather did not sleep together.

But as she turned the handle of the communicating door, she heard his voice and stood still.

It was then she heard a sting of oaths that were more foul than anything she had ever listened to before in her whole life.

A second later she heard the impact of a hand striking flesh and realised he was hitting her mother and she was crying.

Shocked at what she was hearing, Neula was stunned into immobility.

It seemed an eternity of time, while Sir Horace went on swearing and striking her mother again and again.

Then at last she closed the door to get shivering into bed and to lie in the darkness wondering frantically what she could do.

Her mother and father had always been so happy together.

It had never crossed her mind that a man who was a gentleman could treat anyone as lovely and gentle as her mother in such a bestial manner.

She realised, as she felt she should have when she first arrived, that her mother was looking very thin.

The happiness which had once seemed to irradiate her face had gone.

Now she seemed somehow insubstantial, as if her hold on life were a very fragile one.

"What can I do? Oh, God, what can I do?" Neula murmured.

It was a question she was to ask herself all through the next day and the day after.

Tonight, as Neula took her hands from her ears, she could hear once again her mother crying and pleading pitifully:

"Please . . . Horace . . . do not hit me . . . any more!"

"Damn and blast you!" Sir Horace replied furiously. "What is the use of you if you cannot give me what I want? The sooner I am rid of you, the better!"

It was then Neula knew what she must do.

She waited with the door closed for nearly an hour.

When she opened it again very cautiously she was aware, as she expected, that Sir Horace had gone to his own room and her mother was alone.

She could hear her mother sobbing convulsively, and entering the room, Neula felt her way to the bed.

Reaching it, she put out her arms and held her mother close against her.

"It is all right, darling Mama," she said. "I will look after you, and this shall never happen again."

She knew her mother did not understand, and lying down beside her and putting her arms around her, she said:

"Stop crying, Mama, and listen to me. We are going away!"

Her words checked her mother's tears, and after a moment she said:

"I . . . I do not know what you are . . . s-saying."

"I have been thinking it out," Neula replied, "and I feel as if Papa had been guiding and helping me, and telling me what to do."

Her mother gave a little sob that seemed to come from the depths of her heart.

"Oh, darling Charles!" she whispered. "I . . . miss you so! If . . . only I could . . . join you!"

It was something Neula guessed her mother must have longed for over and over again.

"Papa would not wish you to be a coward, Mama," she said, "and I feel, in fact, I know, that he will help us because wherever he is he loves you as he did when he was alive."

"How could he have died . . . when I loved . . . him so?" her mother said brokenly.

"He is not dead," Neula said. "I am quite sure of that!"

"How . . . can you . . . be?"

"When that beastly man was hitting you last night and just now," Neula replied, "I could feel Papa near me."

She paused and smiled at her mother before she went on:

"When I lay in bed wondering how I could save you, he told me quite clearly what we have to do."

Her mother did not reply, but Neula knew she was listening.

"We are going to collect everything we can, then we are going to leave here and go away and hide where Sir Horace will never find us."

"B-but . . . I cannot do . . . that!" her mother objected. "After all, I am his . . . wife!"

"A wife he does not want! A wife he hates!" Neula declared. "If he cannot find you and thinks you are dead, he will thankfully find somebody else to marry!"

There was a silence as she went on:

"We have to be clever about this, Mama. The first thing is to discover when he will be out of the house for long enough for us to get away without his seeing us go."

"You . . . cannot really mean . . . ?" her mother began.

"I mean," Neula said firmly, "to take you somewhere where you will be happy again, and we can be together and forget about Sir Horace, and just remember Papa."

She could almost feel, she thought, hope like a shaft of sunlight running through her mother and lifting her spirits.

"I . . . I am sure it is . . . wrong," Louise said a little feebly.

"I refuse to allow you to stay here and be battered to death by that bully!" Neula flashed. "Anyway, Mama, I could not stay in this house any longer and not tell Sir Horace what I think of him!"

"No . . . no!" her mother cried frantically. "You must not become involved in this, or he might . . . hurt you too!"

"That is certainly something to be avoided," Neula agreed, "so the quicker we get away, the better. Now think, Mama, think when he will be out of the house.'"

Her mother, with what Neula knew was a great effort, wiped her eyes and raised herself a little on the pillows.

"The day after . . . tomorrow," she said in a hesitating voice, "your Stepfather will be . . . leaving, as he is . . . going to London to attend an . . . important dinner."

She took a deep breath before she went on:

"It is for gentlemen only, so he will not want me to . . . accompany him."

"Good!" Neula said. "That means, of course, that he will not be returning for two days."

Neula guessed that after a dinner at which he would have drunk even more than he did ordinarily, Sir Horace would be even more offensive than usual.

She had been surprised at the amount he had drunk both at luncheon and at dinner.

Before leaving for Florence, she had never thought of him as a drinking man.

Now it was obvious that the claret, the champagne, and the port he had imbibed at dinner had inflamed his sense of grievance.

It made him even more brutal towards her mother than he would have been otherwise.

Neula had already seen the bruises on her mother's neck and shoulders when she had gone to her bedroom early in the morning.

Lady Harlow had quickly covered herself with a negligee.

But Neula was certain there were bruises on her breasts and other parts of her body which were evidence of the punishment Sir Horace was inflicting on her.

He was shrewd enough, she had thought, not to hit her mother in the face, where the marks could be seen.

She found herself hating him with an intensity more violent than any emotion she had even known before.

16

"You realise, Mama," she said, "that if we run away, we shall be very poor."

She stopped speaking a moment and then carried on:

"I will find work of some sort, and anything would be better than living in the house watching you suffer at the hands of that madman!"

She knew her mother agreed with her, even though she did not say so, and Neula went on:

"First thing tomorrow you must start thinking of everything you want your maid to pack, so that as soon as Sir Horace leaves the house the next day, there will be very little time wasted before we leave too."

"But . . . where shall we go?" her mother asked in a frightened voice.

"I was thinking," Neula replied, "that if we went back to the village where we lived with Papa, Sir Horace would be bound to look for us there!"

"That is true!" her mother murmured.

"Then just as if Papa were prompting me," Neula went on, "I thought perhaps we might go back to where you lived as a girl, and perhaps find a cottage in the village, where people would be kind to you."

Her mother drew in her breath. Then she said:

"It would be wonderful even to be near my old home. I have thought of it so often, but your father and I never returned there once we had run away."

"Then that is where we shall go!" Neula said. "If we cannot find somewhere to live once we reach Little Bletchley, I am sure there must be lot of other villages."

She paused to smile at her mother before continuing:

"There will be a village where no one would be in the least interested in a widow and her daughter."

"A . . . widow?" her mother asked.

"Of course!" Neula answered. "And although we dare

not call ourselves 'Sherborne,' I thought if you were 'Mrs. Borne,' which is quite an ordinary name, it would be easy for us to remember it!"

Her mother gave a little laugh.

"Oh, darling, you are making it all into a fairy-story! But I am sure when morning comes I shall be sensible enough to know it is impossible."

"What is impossible," Neula contradicted, "is for us to remain here. I am taking you away, Mama, and it is no use arguing about it. That is what is sensible."

"I do not think it is at all sensible," her mother said, "but it would be wonderful not to have to be . . . frightened again and, just as you say . . . think only of . . . Papa."

"Then you have to help me," Neula said, "and first of all, we must have some money."

She could not see her mother as they were lying in the darkness.

Yet she knew her eyes would be wide and questioning as she said in a low voice:

"Money?"

"We cannot live on air," Neula explained as if to a child, "though not at first, but later, when I find work, it will be easier."

"But . . . how can you work? What could you . . . do?" her mother asked.

"If after all that exclusive education I have had," Neula said, "which we both know was very expensive, and the fact that I speak fluent French, Italian, and Spanish, I cannot find some sort of job, then I shall be both surprised and disappointed!"

"But . . . you are a Lady . . . and Ladies do not . . . work!"

"Lady, or no Lady, I do not intend to starve," Neula answered. "So do not let us waste time arguing about it."

She stopped speaking a moment, and then went on:

"Let us concentrate on what we can take which will at least provide us from the start with a roof over our heads, and two good meals a day!"

* * *

Afterwards Neula was to congratulate herself on being very clever in organising the plan for her mother's escape.

First of all, Neula learnt that Sir Horace had a secretary.

She found that he paid the servants' wages as well as the employees who worked on the estate, and every bill went through his office.

It was easy, as soon as Sir Horace had left after breakfast, to approach Mr. Watson.

She told him that she and her mother were invited to stay the night with some friends who lived just the other side of Oxford.

"We shall, of course, need some money for tips and so on," Neula said, "and also, as we are passing through Oxford, my mother is eager to buy me some new clothes to replace those I have been wearing at School."

"Of course, Miss Sherborne," the Secretary replied, "but Her Ladyship has credit at most of the shops."

"Mama told me she seldom goes shopping in Oxford, and that my Stepfather prefers her to buy her clothes in Bond Street," Neula protested.

Mr. Watson realised that was true.

"It would, therefore, be much easier to be able to pay cash than have to wait while they make enquiries as to whether we are respectable," Neula went on, "and not stealing their garments!"

Mr. Watson laughed.

"I am sure they would not think that, Miss Sherborne!"

However, prompted by Neula, and since, as she was

well aware, he thought her a very pretty young girl, he handed over what was, in fact, a remarkably large sum of money.

As he did so he said:

"You will take care of this? I am sure Sir Horace would be horrified to think of so much money lying about!"

"It will be quite safe," Neula assured him, "and I promise you, it will be spent very quickly!"

Mr. Watson laughed again.

"If you take my advice, Miss Sherborne, you will wait until you can go to London. Her Ladyship's clothes come from the best shops in Bond Street."

"And she looks lovely in them!" Neula smiled.

She thought Mr. Watson was going to say that she would look lovely, too, in anything she wore.

As if he thought that would be too familiar, he merely said:

"I hope, Miss Sherborne, you will find exactly what you want."

"I want to look smart for my friends, and smart enough for this house until we can get to London!"

She paused before she added:

"That reminds me! I badly need a travelling-coat. The only one I have makes me look like a School-girl. Perhaps you had better give me another fifty pounds."

As if he were bemused by her, Mr. Watson obliged.

She went up the stairs in triumph to find her mother ready and looking pale and frightened.

Neula kissed her and said:

"Cheer up, Mama! I have managed to extort an astronomical amount of money from Mr. Watson, and with your jewels to sell, we shall be able to live for quite a long time just enjoying ourselves!"

"Oh . . . darling . . . I feel I . . . ought not to g-go!" her mother faltered.

"Well, I am going!" Neula said firmly. "But if you want to stay behind . . ."

Her mother gave a little cry and Neula said quickly:

"I am only teasing you, Mama, and of course you are coming with me, especially after last night!"

She was aware that Sir Horace had then been even more brutal than usual.

She had kept the communicating-door closed, feeling she could not bear to hear her mother being assaulted.

Yet twice there had been screams which had percolated through the heavy mahogany door and made Neula put her head under the sheets.

It was then she had wished, as she never had before, that she had been born a boy.

She would have gone in and given Sir Horace some of his own medicine.

Once again he had been drinking deeply, and only when she was sure he had staggered back to his own room had she gone in to her mother's.

She had made her mother lay out every expensive gown she owned, and also the furs that she wore in the winter, for her lady's-maid to pack.

"Why should Your Ladyship want so many furs when it's getting warmer?" the lady's-maid enquired.

Neula had already anticipated this question and had told her mother what to say.

"My friends with whom I am . . . staying the night," Lady Harlow answered, "tell me they know of a . . . Furrier who can cleverly . . . re-model anything that is . . . out-moded."

She did not lie well.

The colour was coming and going in her face as she spoke, and she was stumbling over the words.

However, her lady's-maid was apparently satisfied.

The carriage in which they travelled was certainly heaped with trunks.

There was even a number of smaller pieces of baggage inside with them.

As they drove away, Neula thought they were setting out on a great adventure.

She was only praying that she had thought of everything and had taken every precaution to avoid Sir Horace discovering where they had gone.

She instructed the coachman to set them down at The Mitre, a well-known coaching Inn in Oxford.

"In order to save Sir Horace's horses from travelling too far," she said loftily, "our friends are sending their carriage to meet us there."

"That's very considerate, Miss," the coachman said.

"That is what I thought too," Neula said lightly.

* * *

Neula and her mother arrived in Oxford at about eleven o'clock.

As soon as the coachman and the footman on the box had left them, Neula enquired which was the best livery stable where she could hire a carriage and horses.

Then they drove until three o'clock, stopping only for a quick luncheon at a Posting-House, where the horses were changed.

Having changed into a different carriage at another Posting-House, they set off again, arriving at Little Bletchley at half-past six in the evening.

It was only now that her mother began to grow nervous that there would be nowhere for them to stay in the village.

She was trying to remember the nearest Inn and finding it difficult, after twenty-one years, to do so.

"Now think, Mama, of somebody who will help us to find a cottage," Neula said. "Perhaps there will be one where we can camp for the night, even if we have to sleep on the floors."

"If Mr. Ainsworth is alive, which I rather doubt," Lady Harlow replied, "he would help us."

"Who is Mr. Ainsworth?"

"He was my father's estate manager. I remember the pensioners all loved him."

She smiled as she added:

"Since they were far too frightened of Papa to complain, they always took their troubles to Mr. Ainsworth."

"Then we will go to find him," Neula said.

She thought her mother looked tired, and taking her hand in hers, she said:

"Do not worry, Mama! As I said before, I know Papa is looking after us."

"Do you really . . . believe that?" her mother asked with hope in her eyes. "I keep talking to him, and somehow I feel I am just . . . imagining that he can . . . hear me."

"Of course he can hear you," Neula said, "and I know he thinks we are doing the right thing."

She smiled at her mother, and then continued:

"I cannot imagine Papa letting any man behave towards you in the way that Sir Horace has!"

"That is . . . true!" Lady Harlow said beneath her breath.

"Just ask Papa to guide us now, and make sure that Mr. Ainsworth is not only alive, but ready to help us."

Lady Harlow gave a little laugh as if she could not help it.

"Oh, Neula, you are so like your father! He was always

sure that everything would turn out for the best, and that 'something would turn up,' as invariably it did!"

"You will see that I am right," Neula prophesized, "or rather that Papa was making you remember Mr. Ainsworth. Now we are going to find him!"

She said a little prayer of her own as she spoke that she was justified in hoping that Mr. Ainsworth would really be there.

Then the carriage in which they were travelling came to a standstill.

The driver bent down towards their open window, shouting:

"Where d'you wanna go?"

Neula looked at her mother.

"The White Cottage at the far end of the village," Lady Harlow told her daughter.

Neula repeated it to the coachman, and as the carriage once again set off, she said:

"Now, Mama, remember you are not Lady Harlow, but Mrs. Borne, and nobody must ever know that we are not who we are pretending to be."

"I will . . . try to remember," her mother said meekly.

"I think Papa would like us to have part of his name."

Neula stopped speaking a moment before continuing:

"If we are pressed, we can always say that we are distant cousins of Lord Borne, and that is why we want to live somewhere in the neighbourhood."

"Oh, Neula, no!" her mother cried. "I shall never remember all these things! Perhaps we are making a mistake, and I ought to go back."

"How can you be so faint-hearted, Mama?" Neula asked. "And remember, we have enough money to stay in hiding for a very long time."

She paused for a moment and then said:

"At least we will not have to rely, like the babes in the wood, on the leaves to cover us."

Lady Harlow gave a little laugh.

Then the horses came to a standstill outside the White Cottage.

chapter two

THE White Cottage was an attractive-looking little house surrounded by its own garden bright with Spring flowers.

Neula looked at it for a moment, then said before she opened the door of the carriage:

"You stay here, Mama. I will see if Mr. Ainsworth is here, and if not, we shall have to go somewhere else."

She did not wait for her mother to reply, thinking she might argue.

She jumped out of the carriage and walked quickly down the pavemented path to the front door.

She knocked and wondered what they should do if there was nobody at home.

After a second or so she heard somebody push back a chair and walk slowly and heavily toward the door.

It opened, and she saw an elderly man with greying hair and what she thought was a kind face.

"Are you Mr. Ainsworth?" she asked.

"I am, and what can I do for you, Ma'am?"

Relieved, Neula said with a smile:

"There is an old friend of yours in a carriage outside who is anxious to see you."

She ran back the way she had come and said to her mother:

"He is there, Mama, and as I like the look of him, I am sure he will help us."

Slowly, as if she were afraid, her mother got out of the carriage and walked to the front door.

For a moment Mr. Ainsworth just stared at her, then he said:

"Miss Louise! I can't believe it!"

"Yes, it is!" her mother answered. "And how are you after all these years?"

She put out her hand as she spoke, and as he took it Mr. Ainsworth said:

"I can hardly believe my eyes! I have thought of you, Ma'am, and was very sorry to hear of Mr. Charles's death."

His words and the kindness in his voice made it impossible for Louise to answer him.

She moved into the cottage as Neula went back to tell the driver of their carriage to wait for them.

"Oi 'opes ye won't be long!" he said in a somewhat surly voice. "Oi wants t'get back afore it's dark!"

"Of course you do," Neula replied, "and I promise you we will be as quick as possible."

He seemed relieved to hear this, and she hurried back into the cottage.

Her mother was sitting in front of the fire in the small but comfortable Sitting-Room, obviously talking over old times with Mr. Ainsworth.

He rose politely to his feet as Neula joined them, and then as she sat down he said:

"I hope you'll forgive me for sitting while we talk, but I had an accident on the farm and have hurt my leg."

"Of course you must sit down!" Louise said quickly. "We will not keep you long."

As she spoke she looked at Neula, who knew that her mother did not wish to explain why they were there and was leaving it to her.

"We have come to you, Mr. Ainsworth, for help," she began.

Looking a little surprised, he did not speak, and she went on:

"My mother and I, for reasons we do not wish to talk about, are in hiding. We wish to rent a small, very cheap cottage, and felt that you might be able to provide us with one."

"But surely, Mrs. Sherborne . . ." Mr. Ainsworth began.

"No, no!" Neula interrupted. "She is not Mrs. Sherborne, and it is very important that she should be spoken of as 'Mrs. Borne.'"

She saw the surprise in his eyes and went on:

"There may be a few people in the village who will remember her, and if they do, you must just explain that she married a very distant cousin of her previous husband and is now Mrs. Borne, which is also my name."

Mr. Ainsworth looked bewildered.

"It is all very complicated," Neula said, "but I am not exaggerating when I say that we have come here to hide."

She paused a moment and then went on:

"We want no one outside the village to have any idea who we are or where we have come from."

Mr. Ainsworth smiled.

"There are not many left who knew Miss Louise when

28

she was a girl. Twenty-one years is a long time, but those that are old enough have long memories."

Neula gave a little laugh.

"That is true, but as they will know her as Mrs. Borne and my name is the same, I feel we shall be safe. So where can we go?"

Mr. Ainsworth looked worried as he said:

"I can't think of any empty cottages available at the moment. There's a very old man called Norton, whom I am sure your mother will remember as he was Butler at the Park, and when he dies . . ."

"We need somewhere at once!" Neula said urgently.

There was silence, and Neula was sure her mother was praying that he would think of somewhere they could go.

Then suddenly his face cleared and he said:

"I have an idea, but I hardly like to propose it to you, Miss Borne."

"I will be grateful to hear anything if it means somewhere we can stay the night," Neula replied.

Mr. Ainsworth's eyes flickered as if he felt embarrassed. Then he said:

"There's one place where nobody would expect you to be and it's empty—the Park!"

For a moment there was silence, then Louise asked nervously:

"Do you mean—my old home?"

Mr. Ainsworth nodded.

"It is like this, Ma'am: when Mr. Hugh lost the house and the estate to the Marquis of Kerne, I was instructed by his Attorney to inspect the property, to look after the estate, and to find caretakers for the house."

Neula drew in her breath, but she did not interrupt as he went on:

"The old servants—all that were left—were pensioned off, and I put Mr. and Mrs. Cossins in as caretakers."

"I remember Cossins," Louise said. "He was the Odd Job Man when I was a girl. He used to clean the boots and do everything about the house that no one else wanted to do."

"That's right, Ma'am," Mr. Ainsworth agreed. "Very useful Cossins was until he was crippled with rheumatism, which with his asthma eventually killed him."

"And Mrs. Cossins?" Louise enquired.

"She died last year, and I've not yet replaced them."

Neula gave a little cry of excitement.

"Are you saying that we could take the Cossins' place and be caretakers at the Park?"

"I was not, of course, suggesting you should do any work," Mr. Ainsworth replied, "but it is empty, and His Lordship is obviously not interested in it."

"But I have to work!" Neula said quickly. "Not immediately, for we have a little money."

She gave a deep sigh and then went on:

"But it will not last for ever, and after I have found somewhere for Mama and me to live, I was going to ask you to find me employment of some sort."

Mr. Ainsworth laughed.

"Well, I do not think being caretakers of the Park would be very arduous, and I am sure I can arrange for somebody from the village to give you a hand with the cleaning now and then."

The way he spoke made Neula feel that he was limited in what he could spend.

As if he knew what she was thinking, Mr. Ainsworth said:

"Although His Lordship has never come near the house

since he won it, every month I receive money for the pensioners, the caretakers, and for the one gardener."

"How could one gardener cope with all there is to do?" Louise expostulated.

"Henry does his best," Mr. Ainsworth said, "but he prefers vegetables to flowers, and I am afraid, Ma'am, you will find the pleasure gardens overgrown, though still very beautiful."

"It will be lovely to see it again," Louise said.

Neula realised there was a touch of excitement in her Mother's eyes as she spoke, which had certainly not been there when they left The Towers.

"We shall be very, very grateful, Mr. Ainsworth, if you will let us caretake in Mama's old home," she said, "and we would also be glad to receive the same wages as you gave the Cossinses."

"No, no, of course not!" Louise interposed, but Neula said quietly:

"We shall need it, Mama, and if the Marquis of Kerne is prepared to pay a caretaker, I personally am not too proud to accept payment for the work I shall certainly do to keep the house in order."

"You are taking on a big task!" Mr. Ainsworth warned.

"But one I am delighted to have!" Neula answered. "Thank you, thank you, for being kind enough not only to find somewhere for us to live, but also to give me employment, which I greatly need."

"It is something I never expected a Tremaine to do, Miss Borne, but I am glad to have been of help."

"You have been a very great help!" Neula said. "Now perhaps you would tell us how we get into the house, because the hired carriage which brought us here is impatient to return to its stable."

"I understand," Mr. Ainsworth smiled, "and I think perhaps in my present state I would be more of a liability than a help."

He stopped speaking to smile at her before he continued:

"I must therefore ask you, Miss Borne, to find your own way into the house and to make what arrangements you please once you are there."

He rose from his chair as he spoke and limped to a desk that was standing in front of the window.

Opening a drawer, he took out a bunch of keys.

One of them was very large, and he said as he gave it to Neula:

"This key opens the back-door. The others are all labelled, and I expect your mother can find her way about the house even better than I can."

* * *

Driving between the ancient oak trees which lined the drive to Tremaine Park, Louise slipped her hand into her daughter's.

She said in a low voice:

"I cannot . . . believe it! I cannot believe I am . . . really going . . . home after all . . . these years!"

"I told you Papa was looking after us," Neula replied. "And I can imagine nothing nicer for you, Mama, than to be in your own home and to forget all the horrible things that have happened to you since he died."

Just for a moment there was a stricken expression in Louise's eyes.

It was always there when she remembered that Charles was no longer with her.

However, she could not repress her excitement as they drove over the stone bridge which spanned the lake.

An incline led to the gravelled courtyard and a flight of stone steps to the front-door.

The coachman obeyed Neula's instructions and turned left.

Passing under an arch, he drove to the back-door, where the kitchens were situated, while a little farther to the right there were the stables.

He drew the horses to a standstill, then, getting down from the box, he said in what Neula thought was a some-what truculent voice:

"Ain't there no 'un to 'elp Oi? All this baggage be too much t'manage on me own!"

"I will help you," Neula said, "but first let me open the door."

She fitted the key into the lock, and as the door opened easily her mother moved quickly past her.

They were in a wide passage with flagged stones, on each side of which Neula guessed were the dairy, the larders, the stillroom, the sculleries, and the kitchen.

Her mother had so often described what her life had been as a girl.

There had been a great number of servants to wait on her father, who liked everything to be uniformly efficient.

Louise hurried down the passage as if to make sure that everything was just as it had always been.

Neula put the keys down on a deal table just inside the door and went outside to help the coachman.

Grumbling as he did so, he carried in their trunks and the larger pieces of luggage.

Neula staggered with the smaller pieces that were inside the carriage.

It made quite a mountain of luggage when they finally got it all into the house.

Then when Neula gave him his fare and a generous tip, he took it without saying "thank you."

He climbed back onto the box, turned his horses, and drove away.

For a moment Neula felt as if she had been left stranded on a desert island with no ship in sight.

Then she told herself that they had been far luckier than she had dared anticipate, and at least her mother would be happy.

She went in search of her, thinking as she did so that it would soon be getting dark.

She had to find some means of lighting the rooms, otherwise they would be groping their way blindly.

She found her mother as she might have expected, in the Drawing-Room which led off the large hall.

Neula could see at once that it was a beautifully proportioned room with a number of high windows looking over the garden.

The furniture was all swathed in Holland covers, but the chandelier was shining in the dying rays of the sun.

There were a number of portraits on the walls.

Blue brocade to match the curtains was inset between white pillars gilded at their tops, where they joined an elaborate pelmet.

Louise was standing at the end of the room, her hands clasped together.

Her daughter thought that the expression of happiness in her face made her look lovely.

She also looked far younger than her thirty-eight years, as young, in fact, as she had looked before she married Sir Horace.

As she heard her daughter behind her, she said in a voice that had a note of rapture in it:

34

"I am home! Oh, darling, I have missed this room where my mother always used to sit."

"I can see it is lovely, just as you always told me it was," Neula said.

As she spoke she slipped her arm through her mother's and said:

"Tomorrow you shall show me all of the house and tell me stories of what you thought and felt before you ran away with Papa."

She smiled at her and then continued:

"But now we have to be practical! Soon it will be dark and whatever you may be able to do, I cannot find my way without candles."

Louise laughed, and it was a happy sound.

"We have something better than candles," she said. "Come, I will show you."

She walked from the Drawing-Room and back towards the kitchen quarters with Neula beside her.

There she went to the Pantry and opened a door next to it.

She then gave a cry of delight as she saw on shelves which reached from the floor to the ceiling that there were a multitude of oil-lamps.

On the other side of the room more shelves containing boxes of candles as well as candle-sticks of all shapes and sizes.

"Good Heavens!" Neula exclaimed as she saw what the room contained.

Louise laughed again.

"My father had everything organised, and as Hugh never lived here, I was sure that everything would be just as Papa ordered it to be until he died."

"It certainly makes things very much easier than I anticipated," Neula said, "and now, having found how we can light our way, suppose you show me our bedrooms? We had better take two lamps with us."

She looked carefully and found that most of the lamps were already filled with oil.

She felt sure there would be further supplies to be found somewhere in that part of the house.

For the moment, however, she was concerned with where they would start.

As Louise led her up the Grand Staircase to the First Floor, she thought how incredibly lucky they were.

If anything could make her mother happy and forget what she had suffered at the hands of Sir Horace, it would be to have come home.

When they reached the landing, Louise hesitated.

"I suppose," she said in a low voice, "as we are only the caretakers, we should sleep in the Servants' Quarters, or at least in the rooms occupied only by unimportant guests."

"Who could be more important than you, Mama?" Neula asked, and her mother laughed.

Then she said, still a little nervously:

"Do you think it would . . . matter if I slept . . . at any rate . . . for tonight in . . . Mama's bedroom?"

"Of course not!" Neula replied. "Show me where it is, and I expect there will be a pleasant room for me next door."

Her mother hurried down the passage as if she felt she might be stopped before she could reach the room where her mother had always been ready to talk to her.

She could remember that when she was in bed she always looked so glamorous and beautiful.

It had seemed impossible when she died that she was no longer there.

As in the rest of the house, the chairs were covered with Holland covers.

Yet the bed with its curtains falling from a golden corola was lovely, as was the painted ceiling above it.

As Neula pulled back the curtains, she could understand why the inlaid furniture, the portrait of Louise as a child over the mantelpiece, and the candelabra fashioned with cupids on either side of the bed meant so much to her mother.

"You sleep here, Mama," she said as Louise just stood looking at everything with a suspicion of tears in her eyes, "and now show me where I am to sleep."

The room next door was almost as beautiful as the one they had just left.

Being practical, Neula made her mother find the linen cupboard where the sheets were stored.

They made up their beds using pillow-cases trimmed with lace which her mother remembered were always kept for best.

"For the moment we are the most important guests, the most distinguished people present, and there is no one to argue about it," Neula smiled.

"I still feel rather . . . guilty," her mother protested, "but as the owner is not interested, why should we care?"

"Why indeed?" Neula answered. "And do not let us think about him, in case our thoughts wing like birds to London and he suddenly has an urge to visit the property he has never seen!"

"Oh, no . . . he must not do that!" Louise cried in horror.

* * *

After eating the sandwiches which Neula had been wise enough to purchase from the inn where they had luncheon, they got into bed.

They were both tired after the journey, having carried upstairs what they required for the night.

37

Neula knew that after what her mother had gone through in the last two years she was in a poor state of health.

Although she did not mention it, she was in pain from the way Sir Horace had treated her last night.

"I must keep her from doing too much," Neula admonished herself. "At the same time, nothing could be better than having something to think about other than Sir Horace."

She said a prayer of gratitude both to God and to her father.

As she fell asleep she was thinking excitedly of all there would be to explore the following day.

*　　*　　*

After a breakfast consisting only of tea without milk, Neula went in search of Henry.

She found him, a stalwart man of about fifty, tending the kitchen-garden.

She could see why Mr. Ainsworth had said he was more interested in vegetables than in flowers.

There was a good crop of vegetables to show for his attentions.

It was, however, still too early in the year to expect that many of them were ready to be eaten.

When she appeared, Henry looked at her in astonishment and she said:

"Good morning! My mother and I have been sent here by Mr. Ainsworth as caretakers, and, as we are new, we are hoping you will be able to help us."

"Oi'll do me best," Henry answered.

"My mother is Mrs. Borne, and I am Neula Borne, and for the moment what we need more than anything else is food!"

Henry looked surprised and Neula went on:

"I want to buy some eggs and perhaps you could tell me how we can manage to get the food we need from the village."

Henry smiled and it made his face look kinder, even while it revealed his broken teeth.

"Oi be a-thinkin'," he said after a moment, "that if ye can droive it, ye could use t'pony an' trap."

Neula repressed a little cry of delight as she asked:

"Are you telling me there are horses here?"

"Aye, there be 'orses, but as there be no one t'ride they, they be turned out in t'paddock. Oi feeds 'em every day. They comes in, o'course, in t'winter."

"I always hoped there would be horses!" Neula said eagerly. "And you say there is a pony-trap?"

"Old Bessy be gettin' on a bit," Henry explained. "But 'er'll tak ye t'village if ye wants me t'put a broidle on 'er."

"It would be very kind if you would."

She hesitated, then she asked:

"Can I buy a few eggs from you?"

"Oi never thought o'sellin' 'em," Henry replied, "but they're jus' comin' on t'lay, an Oi've got plenty."

After that it was easy.

Neula bought a dozen eggs from him, and he told her that milk and butter could be obtained from the Home Farm, which was only a quarter-of-a-mile away across the fields.

"If ye want," he said, "oi'll fetch t'milk and butter fer ye every day, an' ye can go t'village for t'other things."

"I would like to do that in an hour's time," Neula said. "First I am going to cook a few eggs for our breakfast, because my mother and I are both very hungry."

Somewhat shyly Henry offered her some slices of bread and a small pat of butter which she promised to replace after she had been to the village.

Because there was so much to do, they ate in the kitchen at the huge deal table.

There were rafters above them which Louise explained had once hung with hams and sides of bacon.

Neula had got the big stove going after a little trouble, which her mother told her had always had half-a-dozen saucepans on top of it.

Louise had so much to talk about and to explore in the house that she was quite content to let Neula go alone to the village.

On the whole the house was clean, if a little dusty.

Neula was, however, determined, even though it seemed extravagant, that she would ask Mr. Ainsworth for a woman to come regularly and clean the kitchen and the rooms they wished to use.

After all, she was sure while they had no rent to pay, the money provided by Mr. Watson would last a long time.

She had not forgotten the value of her mother's jewellery.

It came to her mind when she opened the safe in the Pantry to put in the bulk of their money and found it was packed with silver, most of it put away tidily in green baize covers.

"I am putting our money here for safety, Mama," she said, "and you had better fetch your jewellery. It would be a mistake to leave it lying about, even if there is no one but ourselves in the house."

There was a little pause, then Louise said in a low voice:

"I . . . I did not . . . bring it."

Neula, who was looking at the stove, straightened herself and enquired:

"What do you mean—you did not bring it?"

"I ... I left it behind. Please ... please, Neula, do not be ... angry with me."

"But why? We agreed it would be a safeguard against the future."

"I know ... dearest, and I suppose it was ... stupid of me ... but I could not bear to take anything that ... Sir Horace had given me ... thinking I could give him ... something in ... return."

Louise stumbled over the words and Neula could understand what she was saying.

She was, however, horrified that now they had very much less money to support them than she had anticipated.

"I am ... sorry ... oh ... Neula ... I am sorry ... when you have been so ... kind," her mother said. "Perhaps it was ... selfish of me ... but I could not ... bear to feel I had brought away anything so valuable as the ... jewels when he ... h-hated me!"

As she spoke, tears ran down her mother's cheeks and Neula moved swiftly to put her arms around her.

"It is all right, Mama," she said comfortingly. "Do not cry. I understand, and, of course, you were right. Only somebody as good and as sensitive as you would have behaved in such a way."

"You are ... not angry?" Louise asked.

"Of course not," Neula replied, "and we will manage. Of course we will manage! How could we do anything else, when Papa is looking after us?"

Louise's eyes were swimming with tears, but she looked happy as she said:

"You sound just like your ... father when you ... talk like that ... and I was so ... afraid you would be ... furious with me ... and think I was very ... stupid."

"I not only love, but admire you, Mama," Neula said, and kissed her.

Only when she was driving alone to the village did she wonder how long the money she had with her would last.

It had cost a considerable amount to hire the carriage which had brought them to Little Bletchley.

There would be the wages they would receive for care-taking, although Neula was certain it would be little more than a few shillings a week.

One consolation was they had a large amount of clothes which would last them a long time.

Although many of them might seem very unsuitable for caretakers, there would be nobody to see them, so it would not really matter what they wore.

"It is no use looking too far ahead!" Neula admonished herself as Bessy plodded slowly down the drive, refusing to hurry.

That was an easy thing to say.

Only after she had shopped at the Grocer's, buying in a little store of things they would need such as salt, tea and bread, rice, sugar, and flour, she found herself reluctantly counting each penny she had expended.

It was the first drawing from what she knew was their precious capital and, when that was spent, there would be no more.

She was aware that the people to whom she talked in the village were very curious.

When she explained that she and her mother were the caretakers of what they referred to as the "Big House," they wanted to know who they were and where they came from.

"Ye don' look loik a caretaker t'me, Miss," the Grocer said.

He was obviously a very garrulous man, and Neula was sure all the gossip in the village circulated round him.

"Well, that is what I am," Neula said lightly, "and my

mother and I will look after the house with great care. I am sure you are all very proud of it."

"Us was when t'General were alive," the Grocer replied, "but things be different now, an' it bain't t'same when there is no Lady or Gentleman, so to speak, alivin' there."

"That's true enough!" a woman who was listening chimed in. "I were only sayin' to my 'Ubby t'other night —it gives you the creeps, it do!"

She gave a snort and then continued:

"A great 'ouse like that standin' empty, an' nothin' but the mice moving in it!"

Neula laughed.

"Well, my mother and I are there now, but I agree there will not be the parties or the visitors . . . as there were in the General's time."

"They gives us somethin' t'talk about, they did!" a woman said. "An' we often used to talk of 'ow the General's daughter, Miss Louise, eloped! Real romantic, it were. Now, I s'pose they be nothin' but ghosts."

"Yer be too imaginative, Mrs. Bates, that's wot yer be!" the Grocer said. "An' this young woman as says she's the caretaker don't look nothin' loik a ghost t'me!"

Neula laughed.

"No, indeed! And thank you very much for helping me. I hope I have forgotten nothing."

"If ye 'as, Oi'll be 'ere tomorrow!" the Grocer said.

"No mistake about that!" Mrs. Bates said jokingly. "An' as ye well know, there's no one else we can go to."

"Wot ye're asayin' is whatever I charges yer 'as to pay!" the Grocer parried.

As this was a familiar joke, both he and Mrs. Bates laughed uproariously.

Neula left them, thinking that, as Little Bletchley was

so isolated from the outside world, it was very much to her mother's advantage.

She was sure that not only would Sir Horace fail to find them, but it was quite likely he would not even wish to do so.

As her mother had said, he hated her.

Driving back to the Park, Neula began to plan that perhaps in a year or so they could somehow give him grounds for believing that her mother was dead.

Then they would be free and no longer feel that he overshadowed them.

Having a vivid imagination, Neula always made everything she did into a fairy-story.

Although she had never dreamt that she would find such a haven as Tremaine Park for them to live in, she could not stop her mind rushing ahead.

She tried to plot out the course of the future.

Just as she planned what they would do tomorrow, so she tried to make it fit into place like a jig-saw puzzle.

"When we are settled," she told herself, "and no longer afraid of Sir Horace, perhaps I can find friends for Mama, because otherwise she will be very lonely."

She remembered how amusing it had been when her mother and father entertained the gentlemen who came to buy her father's horses, or the few neighbours who lived nearby.

It was impossible to offer any of them extravagant hospitality.

But the mere fact that they were so young and happy and obviously so very much in love seemed to the people who joined them an entertainment in itself.

Looking back, Neula thought that they always seemed reluctant to leave.

It was almost as if they could not bear to tear themselves

away from the small house that seemed to vibrate with laughter and with love.

"Mama must live that sort of life again," she told herself.

She remembered how she had thought, when she was in Florence, of her mother being provided with every luxury, every material comfort, by Sir Horace.

Instead of which, it had been a nightmare of horror and violence which was something her mother could not stand up to.

It would have left scars which Neula knew would never completely heal.

"I have to look after Mama now and make her happy," she told herself as Bessy moved a little faster towards where her stable was waiting.

She felt that her mother was more like a child than a parent.

It was she who would have to make all the decisions in the future.

"But you will have to help me, Papa!" she said in her heart as Bessy drew up outside the back-door. "You have been splendid up to now, so please do not fail me!"

chapter three

THE Marquis of Kerne sat back in his chair and stared at the Prime Minister in astonishment.

"Are you seriously telling me that I am banished?" he asked.

"It is more a question of being stood in a corner," the Prime Minister replied, "and only for three months."

"However you put it, it is a damned insult!" the Marquis exclaimed.

"I agree with you, Kerne," Earl Grey replied, "but there is nothing you can do about it."

"If Prince Kluchusky had any decency, he would have called me out like any other man!" the Marquis said angrily.

"I believe he did consider it," Earl Grey replied, "but the King, as you know, has denounced duelling."

He paused and then continued:

"He actually told me you were not to insult the representative of a foreign country by even thinking of such a solution to the problem."

"This is Queen Adelaide's doing!" the Marquis protested. "Men have been settling their differences in a gentleman-like manner for centuries, and why should she interfere?"

Earl Gray made a helpless gesture with his hands as he said:

"I am sorry, Kerne, and I have every sympathy for you, but the King's wish, or rather command, if you like, is that you are not to be seen at Court or in London for the next three months."

He made a somewhat wry grimace as he added:

"It is not particularly pleasant for me to have to tell you this."

"It is not particularly pleasant for me to hear it!" the Marquis snapped.

It was, in fact, like a bomb-shell for the Marquis of Kerne.

He was noted for his love-affairs, if that was the right word for them, with all the most attractive women in London.

In the reign of George IV he had been admired and envied for his amatory prowess.

Although husbands ground their teeth when they saw him and swore revenge, they were usually too chicken-livered to challenge him when he was a noted shot and outstanding swordsman.

But as the Marquis knew himself, times had changed with the death of George IV and the Coronation of his brother, William.

King William had led a somewhat chequered career himself, with ten illegitimate children by the actress Mrs. Jordan.

Now, since he married Queen Adelaide, who at the time was only twenty-five to his fifty-three years, everything had changed, mostly, many of the Courtiers thought, for the worse.

First there had blown a cold wind of economy over the court, which presented a very different picture from King George's wild extravagance and personal desire for luxury.

King William saved fourteen thousand pounds a year by dismissing his brother's German Band and replacing it with an English and very much less skillful one.

He sacked the French Chef who had followed his predecessor from residence to residence.

This was an economy daily deplored by those who ate at the Royal table.

Lord Dudley, who was celebrated for his *sotto voce* remarks, grumbled:

"What a change to be sure! Cold pâtés and hot champagne!"

Everywhere the luxurious structure of the late King's way of life was dismantled.

The Royal yachts were cut down to two from five, and George's delightful and sumptuous cottage at Windsor was practically demolished.

Worst of all, the Royal Stud was reduced to half its former size.

Besides all this, in place of its previous most enjoyable impropriety, the Court became parochially Puritan and just as dull.

In a way it was strange that Queen Adelaide should be prim and proper about the behaviour of everybody with whom she and the King associated.

At the same time, she accepted his illegitimate children with commendable broad-mindedness.

It was obvious, the Prime Minister thought now, looking

across his desk, that sooner or later the Marquis of Kerne would come up against the Queen.

To put it bluntly, she was determined there should be no scandals, no clandestine assignations, no adultery at Court.

It was therefore inevitable that some husband who had been cuckolded by the Marquis would be astute enough to enlist the Queen's indignation on his behalf.

Looking at the Marquis sitting opposite him, the Prime Minister thought it would be difficult for any man to look more handsome or more attractive to women.

Therefore, it was not only his looks, his height, the breadth of his shoulders, and the narrowness of his hips which were outstanding.

He was also a superb rider, an outstanding sportsman, whose horses were first past the winning-post in every classic.

Besides all this, he was extremely intelligent.

When he chose to stir himself, the Marquis could make a better speech in the House of Lords than any of his contemporaries could.

It was unfortunately only too true that he was just as compelling to those who listened to him when he was making love.

Before the Marquis had come to his office, the Earl had amused himself by recalling the numerous love-affairs in which he was known to have been involved in the last few years.

He soon gave up counting.

He thought, instead, that no other man could have collected the hearts of so many beautiful and alluring women without the special magnetism which the Marquis undoubtedly possessed.

Yet now, perhaps for the first time in his life, he had

come up against an obstacle that he could not ignore with a shrug of his shoulders.

It was not only the fact of being corrected, or, rather, punished that was so irksome, it was also, Earl Grey thought, the ignominy of being sent away from Court like a small boy being expelled from School.

As if the Marquis were thinking the same thing, he asked sharply:

"Who else knows about this?"

"At the moment only myself," the Prime Minister replied. "His Majesty sent for me early this morning, and told me what I was to say to you, and because I am fond of you, Kerne, I have no intention of gossiping about it."

"I am grateful," the Marquis replied, "and do you think we can rely on Her Majesty not to talk to her Ladies-in-Waiting?"

"I think we can," the Prime Minister replied. "Her Majesty's sense of duty is one of her best qualities."

He paused a moment and then went on:

"Brought up in a narrow-minded provincial Court, she has a very clear idea of the principles by which life ought to be governed and has no intention of modifying her views to suit England."

The Marquis laughed but he did not interrupt, and Earl Grey went on:

"I heard somebody remark yesterday that Her Majesty is the sort of woman who every man maintains would make an excellent wife for somebody else!"

The Marquis laughed again.

"What I am really saying," the Prime Minister continued, "is that so far, and I am sure it is ingrained in her, she has not been known to gossip, especially if it involved being unkind."

"That is what I want to hear," the Marquis said, "and I

shall make every endeavour, if you will kindly be equally punctilious, to give nobody the impression that I have been banished."

"You will be back in time for Royal Ascot," the Prime Minister said consolingly.

"I hope so, as I intend to win the Gold Cup!"

When he left the Prime Minister, it was with a jaunty air, as if he had not a care in the world.

Only when he climbed into his Phaeton, which was waiting for him outside, and took up the reins did he think with fury that the Queen and Prince Kluchusky between them had made a fool of him.

He hoped to God that none of his friends, or his enemies, would be aware of it.

He knew only too well that the story would run like wildfire through the houses in Mayfair and the Clubs in St. James's.

There would be tears from many pairs of eyes he had beguiled.

These would certainly be offset by smirks of satisfaction on their husband's faces.

"Damn it! Damn it!" the Marquis swore to himself as he tooled his horses with an expertise which was the envy of every member of the "Four-in-Hand" Club.

When he drew up outside his house in Berkeley Square, the Marquis handed the reins to his groom.

He then walked into the hall in a manner which made four footmen and a Butler know apprehensively that he was in one of his "black" moods.

Their well-trained, impassive faces, however, gave no sign of it as the Marquis said sharply:

"Send Mr. Carstairs to me immediately!"

"Very good, M'Lord," the butler answered.

By the time the Marquis had poured himself a glass of

champagne and sat down at his desk, Mr. Carstairs came into the room.

He was a middle-aged man with a habitually worried expression.

The Marquis knew that the running of his houses and estates to the standard of perfection he demanded was due to Mr. Carstairs's near-genius as an administrator.

In fact, the two men complemented each other.

Mr. Carstairs would carry out the Marquis's ideas exactly as he required, and in some ways they almost thought alike.

Because Mr. Carstairs had been with him for ten years, the Marquis had few secrets from him.

He was well aware that the older man had as well as a respect a genuine affection for him.

As Mr. Carstairs crossed the room, the Marquis said frankly:

"I am in trouble, Carstairs!"

"I was afraid you might be, My Lord."

"How could you possibly anticipate that?" the Marquis asked in surprise.

There was a little hesitation before Carstairs replied:

"His Highness Prince Kluchusky has the reputation of being a violent man, and he is, in fact, very Russian."

The Marquis gave a little laugh that had no humour in it.

"You size it up very well, but the Prince has not, as I am sure you expected, challenged me to a duel."

Mr. Carstairs raised his eye-brows.

"No, My Lord?"

"He has been cleverer than that, blast him! He merely complained to Her Majesty the Queen and she has done the rest."

Mr. Carstairs gave a gasp. Then he said:

"That is very grievous news, My Lord, very grievous!"

"You can imagine what I am feeling," the Marquis said. "And the one thing I do not want is that every idiot whom I have beaten on the race-course, taken money off at the card-tables, or snubbed for being impertinent should crow over me like a cock on top of a dung-hill!"

There was a little pause before Mr. Carstairs said:

"I can understand that, My Lord."

"The Prime Minister says he will not talk and I can trust him, and I think the King is fond of me in his own way."

He paused a moment, and then continued:

"If he remembers his own chequered career, he will have some understanding of my predicament and will keep his mouth shut."

There was defiance in the Marquis's eyes as he said:

"What we have to do, Carstairs, is to find some reasonable explanation for my leaving London."

He paced up and down before he went on:

"We must discover a place to which I can go which will not seem too surprising, considering racing is just starting and I should be at Newmarket next week."

"You do not intend to go there, My Lord?"

"And have everybody enquiring why I have not accepted their invitations in London?" the Marquis asked.

There was silence. Then Mr. Carstairs, who was obviously thinking hard, said:

"I suppose Your Lordship could go abroad!"

"That is the last thing I can do!" the Marquis answered. "To go abroad at this moment would convince everybody that I was in trouble, and inevitably point to Princess Natalia."

"That is true," Mr. Carstairs agreed. "To be frank, My Lord, I must tell you there has been a great deal of gossip,

53

in view of her remarkable beauty and the large number of ladies who are very jealous of her!"

The Marquis knew this was true.

There had been tears and recriminations from several English beauties who believed the Princess had supplanted them in his affections, which, in fact, she had.

It had been impossible for him not to be intrigued and amused by her.

She was not only one of the most fascinating women he had ever met, but certainly the most seductive.

She had attracted him from the moment they first met.

She had then set out to entice him with an originality and expertise which he found extremely intriguing.

With her Royal blood, of which she was immensely proud, she could be, if she wished, very much the *"Grande Dame"* in public.

In private she was as fierce as a leopardess, and the Marquis had never known a woman who was more wildly aroused when he made love to her.

He was used to the complacency of English husbands who, on the whole, found it easier to look the other way when he was pursuing, or, equally often, being pursued by their wives.

He therefore had underestimated the fury of the Russian, who considered his behaviour a deadly insult.

The Prince was attached temporarily to the Russian Embassy and therefore enjoyed diplomatic immunity.

Also because it was politically expedient to be friendly with Russia, the Marquis had, symbolically, stirred up a hornet's nest.

Mr. Carstairs sighed and his eyes were very worried indeed.

He knew much better than anyone else how humiliating

it would be if it became known that the Marquis had been reprimanded by the King and Queen.

In fact, more or less "sent to Coventry" until he learned to behave himself.

"Come on, Carstairs!" the Marquis said. "You must have some ideas. Where else have I houses that I can visit except at Newmarket, where everybody will see me."

He stopped speaking and thought for a moment before he went on:

"Or what about Leicestershire when it is not the hunting season?"

"You do not think, My Lord, that if you went to Kerne House in Buckinghamshire it would appear that you had to concern yourself with local affairs?"

"What would happen then would be that a large number of my friends would invite themselves to stay, and when they returned to London they would expect me to go with them."

"Yes, of course, My Lord, I understand."

Mr. Carstairs thought for a moment. Then he said:

"There is, of course, Tremaine Park, which Your Lordship has never visited."

"Tremaine Park?" the Marquis repeated. "Where the devil is that?"

"You must remember, My Lord," Mr. Carstairs replied, "that you won it at cards over a year ago from Mr. Hugh Tremaine, who was later killed in a duel in France."

"Good Heavens! I had forgotten all about it!" the Marquis exclaimed.

He paused a moment whilst he tried to recall the incident.

"I remember him!" he carried on. "He was a stupid young man who drank too much, and went on gambling when he had no possible hope of winning!"

"You will recall, My Lord, that he lost his house and estate to you, but as you have never showed any interest in it, I just left it in the hands of the Estate Manager."

"Where is it?" the Marquis asked.

"It is in Hertfordshire, near Potters Bar, where, you will remember, your Lordship went once to a Horse Fair."

"What is it like?" the Marquis asked.

"From all I have heard, it is a very fine example of early Georgian architecture with an estate of three thousand acres, on which the rents are low."

"And you say it belonged to Hugh Tremaine?"

"Yes, and before that to his father, General Sir Alexander Tremaine," Mr. Carstairs replied.

"I seem to have heard the name," the Marquis said. "But what is to be my excuse to the household there for suddenly arriving?"

"I am sure there is a great deal of re-organisation there to be done, and no one here will know where Your Lordship has gone."

"It is an idea!" the Marquis said grudgingly. "But where will you tell my friends I am?"

"I think, My Lord, it might be a good idea to tell them that there had been a fire in your castle in Scotland and there was nothing you could do but leave at once to see what could be saved from the ruins."

"That sounds quite plausible," the Marquis said, "and quite a number of men have stayed with me in Scotland."

"I am sure they will be very sorry, My Lord, to hear of a fire in such a fine Castle!"

The Marquis gave a short laugh without any humour in it.

"That is as good a plan as any other," he said, "and as I have no wish to answer any questions, I will leave at once for—what did you say it was called?—Tremaine Park."

Mr. Carstairs looked at him in consternation.

"My Lord, you cannot do that! The house is shut up except for the caretakers."

"As I shall not need the staff here for three months," the Marquis said, "send what servants I shall need there down in the brake with the luggage. I will, of course, take both chefs with me."

He added angrily:

"If I have to go to the country, I am damned if I am going to eat nothing but boiled beef and carrots!"

He rose to his feet as he spoke, drank what was left of the champagne in his glass, and said:

"I will go to change. Tell them to bring Pegasus round in half-an-hour."

He walked from the room as he spoke, and Mr. Carstairs stared after him in some anxiety.

Too late, he wished he had taken more trouble over Tremaine Park in the past, or at least had gone down himself to see what it was like.

He was quite certain that since it had been left empty for well over two years, the Marquis would find it intolerably uncomfortable.

But he knew there was no use in trying to dissuade the Marquis from leaving immediately, for once he had made up his mind, it was impossible for anybody to change it.

Mr. Carstairs therefore hurried to find the Butler and the housekeeper, as well as the Chefs, to galvanise them all into an unprecedented activity.

*   *   *

The Marquis set off alone precisely half-an-hour later.

He was looking, Mr. Carstairs had to admit, so smart and so dashing that it seemed almost a crime that he should

57

be buried in the country instead of enlivening the London scene.

Only he knew what the Marquis was feeling underneath his air of supreme indifference.

A self-control which he had to admire made him say in front of the servants:

"If anybody enquires for me, tell them I am performing a wearisome duty."

"I will do that, My Lord," Mr. Carstairs replied, knowing that the servants who were going to Tremaine Park with the Marquis must have an explanation for the sudden upheaval.

He was aware also that he must give a very different explanation to those who were to learn that His Lordship had gone to Scotland.

As the Marquis rode out of London, he found the sun was shining.

The trees were coming into bud, the grass was green, and there were primroses in the hedgerows, all of which made him begin to feel a little more cheerful.

But mostly it was due to the horse he was riding, a magnificent black stallion which he had bought six months ago at Tattersall's.

He knew it was worth every penny of the large sum he had paid for it.

A superb rider, he preferred travelling alone, even though it would have been more usual to take a groom with him.

He had found on previous journeys that unless the man was on a perfectly matched horse to his own, he was apt to lag behind.

Anyway, at the moment he had no wish for anybody's company except his own.

He knew the way to Potters Bar, as Mr. Carstairs had implied.

He had been twice to the Horse Fair which took place every year.

On one occasion he had bought a yearling at a reasonable sum which had won many races for him.

He learnt that Little Bletchley was about four miles farther on.

After having had luncheon at a passable Posting Inn, he set off to discover the village and Tremaine Park.

At about three o'clock in the afternoon he turned in at some wrought-iron gates with a lodge on either side of them.

He thought the long vista of oak trees looked quite encouraging.

Then, as he rode on and saw the house ahead of him, he knew Mr. Carstairs had been right.

It was indeed an excellent example of early Georgian architecture and, as such, very attractive.

He crossed the bridge spanning the lake.

He paused for a minute in the centre of it to look down at two swans moving serenely towards a small cascade at the far end.

It was certainly beautiful.

He told himself that if he had to endure solitary confinement on the King's orders for three months, it would be hard to find a more pleasant place in which to do so.

At the same time, he was aware that the garden was overgrown, although the shrubs were coming into bloom, as were the fruit trees growing beside the lake.

He drew up his horse outside the grey stone steps.

He saw to his surprise that the front door was open, when he had expected it to be closed and barred.

He had intended to take his horse to the stables, but on an impulse he thought he would enter the house first.

As it was unlikely there would be any food for Pegasus in the stables until his grooms arrived, he might as well enjoy what grass he could find.

The Marquis had already taught the stallion to come when he was called.

He now dismounted, knotted the reins on Pegasus's neck, and left him free.

He knew because it had been quite a long journey and the horse was tired, he would not wander far.

Then the Marquis walked up the steps.

He thought it was quite an adventure to enter a house which he owned but which had completely slipped his memory until a few hours ago.

He reached the top of the steps.

Then he stopped for a moment to look back at the lake below him and at the oak trees in the Park.

Already his mind was busy thinking what improvements he could make.

Finally he turned and walked into an attractive marble hall.

There was a carved staircase on one side of it, and a very fine marble fireplace on the other.

There were portraits on the wall which he supposed were of the Tremaine ancestors.

It struck him that everything seemed clean and well-polished when he had expected to find dust and cobwebs.

There was a double door at the far end of the hall, one half being open.

He walked towards it, realising as he did so that the room it led into was not shuttered and the sunshine was pouring in through the windows.

He had a quick impression of white and blue walls, a crystal chandelier, and sconces guttering in the sunlight.

Then he saw at the far end of the room, standing in the window arranging some flowers, there was a young woman.

She had her back half-turned to him and as she heard him she said:

"Do look! The first white lilac and it smells absolutely lovely!"

"I am glad to hear that!" the Marquis said.

The young woman turned swiftly, and he was looking into a small, pointed face in which were two huge eyes now wide with astonishment at the sight of him.

Above them were little red curls that seemed to dance in the sunshine on a golden head.

* * *

Neula rode back early in the morning towards the house.

She thought she had spent ten days of perfect happiness since she and her mother had come to Tremaine Park.

It had been a joy beyond words to find that the horses that had been put out to grass were well-bred.

They were, in fact, exactly what would have pleased her father had he been able to afford them.

They had, of course, become somewhat wild and unmanageable through lack of exercise.

She would not have been her father's daughter if she did not know how to handle a horse.

It took her several days of determined struggle and two or three falls before she finally had one horse completely under control.

Now she was breaking in another for her mother.

She had been very firm in making Louise rest as much

61

as possible and not do much during the first days at Tremaine Park.

It was not only what she had suffered physically at the hands of Sir Horace that had upset her.

It was also her uneasy feeling that she had done something wrong in running away.

Neula reassured her over and over again that she had done the only thing possible.

Things were made much easier after she had visited Mr. Ainsworth again.

He told her he was sending a village woman called Amy up to the house every morning to clean the rooms that had been neglected, and to scrub the kitchen-quarters.

"I am afraid we cannot afford it, Mr. Ainsworth," Neula had said firmly when he first suggested it.

"You are not to worry about that, Miss Neula," Mr. Ainsworth had replied, "first, because I have nearly six months wages in hand of which I have spent very little while no caretaker has been permanently installed."

He saw the delight in Neula's eyes and went on:

"Secondly, I would have no compunction, if you find it impossible even with Amy's help to manage in the house, asking His Lordship's secretary for a rise in your wages."

Neula laughed. Then she said:

"It is very kind of you, but the one thing we do not want is to draw attention to ourselves."

She paused and then continued:

"I am sure we can manage with Amy, and when you have expended on her wages all the money you have spare, you must tell me."

"I feel very embarrassed," Mr. Ainsworth replied, "that there is so little for Miss Lou . . . I mean your mother and yourself."

"We are very happy and content," Neula said. "I cannot

tell you how wonderful it is for Mama to feel she has come home!"

She paused, then as if she felt it only fair to Mr. Ainsworth, she explained:

"She has been very unhappy since my father died, and her second marriage was a disaster."

"I somehow sensed that," Mr. Ainsworth said, "so we must do everything to see that she is comfortable and happy here."

"That is what I want to do," Neula said.

"And you are quite right," he continued, "we do not want His Lordship to become interested in Tremaine Park!"

The way he spoke made Neula look at him curiously and ask:

"Tell me about the Marquis."

"What I have heard is certainly not for your ears, Miss Neula!"

"Why not? And how do you know anything about him if he never comes here?"

"Well, it is like this," Mr. Ainsworth began. "When Mr. Hugh went to London, he took with him as a valet one of the footmen, a young man who lived in the village."

He stopped speaking to smile at Neula before continuing:

"He is a good lad who comes from decent stock, and to put it bluntly, Miss Neula, he was shocked by your uncle's behaviour and looked for another job."

"And got one, I suppose, with the Marquis," Neula said.

"How did you guess?" Mr. Ainsworth exclaimed.

"It is the sort of coincidence that could happen only in a fairy-story, which is what we are living," Neula answered. "But do go on!"

"Well, Billy, as he is always called, came home occasionally, and then when Mr. Hugh lost the house to the Marquis, naturally all the village were very curious about him."

Mr. Ainsworth paused, and Neula protested:

"You cannot stop there!"

"I am trying to think how I can put it politely," Mr. Ainsworth answered. "The Marquis is well known as an owner on the race-course and is an exceptional rider himself."

He shook his head.

"But the stories of his private life in London are very lurid and not for your ears."

"What you are saying," Neula said, "is that the Marquis has had a great number of love-affairs."

She thought Mr. Ainsworth looked a little shocked, and she explained:

"I was educated in Florence, Mr. Ainsworth, and I have listened to the Italian girls, the French girls, and the Spanish girls."

She gave a little giggle.

"They all talk about love from first thing in the morning until last thing at night!"

She smiled and then went on:

"They regaled me with the love-affairs of their brothers, their cousins, their fathers, and, I suspect, their grandfathers!"

Mr. Ainsworth laughed as if he could not help it. Then he said:

"You are too young to know about that sort of thing, Miss Neula."

"At the moment I feel very old because I have to look after Mama."

"And I suppose you can look after yourself," Mr. Ainsworth remarked with a smile.

"I think so, and after all, we have done very well up to now, first by running away, then in finding you."

She knew as she spoke that she had made a mistake and said quickly:

"I am trusting you, Mr. Ainsworth, and I feel you will not let me down."

"I can promise you, Miss Neula, I would do anything in my power to help Miss Louise."

He paused a moment before adding:

"If you enjoy being here, it is only half as much as I enjoy being able to help you both!"

Because he was obviously so sincere, it made Neula feel all the happier.

She felt there need never be any reason for them to leave the Park, and perhaps in the future they would be able to make a few friends.

When she reached the stable she put her horse into his stall, knowing that Henry would rub him down for her.

There was already clean straw on the floor, and the bucket was filled with fresh water.

She wished she could tip Henry for all he had done for them since they had arrived.

But she was still very eager not to touch any of the money which was in the safe.

She was, in fact, trying to spend nothing but their wages as caretakers, which she was sure would be only a few shillings, on buying their food.

She had discovered that there were fat young pigeons in the woods and fields and that two men in the village had guns.

She paid them a few pennies for each pigeon they brought her and gave the same to the small boys who snared rabbits in the Park.

They were delighted to have a little money of their own to spend on buying sweets at the Grocer's.

"We will manage, we can manage for quite a long time!" Neula told herself optimistically.

She ran into the house to let her mother know that she was back.

"I have started to cook luncheon, dearest," Louise said from the kitchen.

"I will come to help you in a moment," Neula answered, "but I want to change after riding."

"I have put one of my gowns on your bed," Louise replied. "I thought, dearest, what you were wearing yesterday looked a little tight."

Neula was about to ask what did it matter when there was nobody to see her, then thought it would be a mistake.

She wanted her mother to take an interest in everything, including herself, so she merely said:

"Thank you, Mama darling. I am sure that Henry, when I see him, will appreciate how smart I look!"

Louise laughed as Neula had meant her to do, but as her daughter's footsteps died away down the passage she gave a little sigh.

If Neula was worried about the future, so was she.

She was well aware that at eighteen Neula should be making her curtsy at Buckingham Palace and meeting young people of her own age.

Especially eligible young men, one of whom she might wish to marry.

"I am being selfish, terribly selfish!" Louise said as she stirred the sauce in the pan.

Then she remembered how Sir Horace had met her.

Now his ardour had changed until she had known that he hated her with an unsuppressed violence because she could not give him what he most wanted.

She shuddered and told herself that however much she loved her daughter, she could not go back and face such purgatory again.

"Something must be done sooner or later," she murmured beneath her breath. "Please, Charles darling, find a solution! I feel so utterly and completely helpless without you!"

Tears came into her eyes and she brushed them away as she heard Neula coming down the passage.

As her daughter came into the room, Louise lifted the plates out of the oven and she put them on the table.

Then she realised that Neula was standing with her arms held out elegantly and one foot pointing daintily as she posed in the gown she was wearing.

"Look, Mama!" she said. "The chrysalis has turned into a butterfly, and every man I meet is falling on his knees at the sight of me!"

Louise laughed.

She thought that Neula was indeed looking very lovely in a gown of very pale blue gauze which she had always thought was a little too young for herself.

"You look lovely, darling!" she exclaimed. "Now, come and sit down and eat your luncheon while it is hot."

"What have we on the menu today?" Neula enquired.

"Henry insisted on killing one of his hens for us. I boiled it, and I shall be disappointed if it is not very tender."

"What I am really looking forward to," Neula said, "is one of his young chickens, but I doubt if he will let us have one."

"I am certain he will keep them for laying, so that he can sell us the eggs," her mother replied.

Neula told her mother what she had seen and done out

riding, and they laughed and talked until their luncheon was finished.

Then having washed up the dishes, Neula said:

"And now, Mama, you are to go and rest! Amy turned out your mother's *Boudoir* yesterday, so I know you will be comfortable in the window on the *chaise longue*."

"You spoil me," Louise said, "but because I know you will argue if I refuse, I will do as you say."

"You are to try to go to sleep," Neula insisted, "and I am going into the garden to pick some flowers. Then we will have tea in the Drawing-Room as you used to do, with the Queen Anne tea-service."

She paused before she added:

"We will pretend that at least two Dukes and perhaps a few Earls are popping in to join us!"

Louise was laughing as she went up the stairs, and picking up a basket and a pair of scissors, Neula went into the garden.

She knew it pleased her mother when there were plenty of flowers in the house as there had been when she was a girl.

Actually, she much enjoyed arranging them, thinking a little wistfully, as she did so, of the empty greenhouses.

Henry had told her they once housed orchids, malmaison carnations, and many other hot-house flowers.

She told herself a story of how by some miracle they had enough money to employ five or six gardeners.

They would make the gardens look as they had been when her mother was a girl.

It made her think, as she arranged the white lilac which had just come into bloom, that it was very like her mother —lovely, fragile, and fragrant!

Then she heard her come into the room.

"Do look!" she said. "The first white lilac and it smells absolutely lovely!"

It was when a man's voice answered her that she turned round.

Standing staring at her was the most elegant, the most handsome man she had ever seen.

For a moment he seemed to be just a figment of her imagination, part of the story she had been telling herself.

She had thought of the house filled with people, with footmen in the hall and a number of attentive maid-servants upstairs.

Then she realised the newcomer was real.

Although he looked as if he might have stepped out of a fairy-story, he was, in fact, a living man, and she asked in a rather nervous voice:

"Who are . . . you?"

"I think that is the question I should be asking you!" the Marquis replied as he walked towards her. "I understood that my house was empty!"

"*Your* house?" Neula gasped. "Then you are the . . . Marquis of Kerne!"

"I am! And now perhaps you will explain who you are!"

For a moment Neula was so bemused that she almost told him the truth. Then she said with difficulty:

"I . . . I am Neula . . . Borne . . . one of your . . . new care-takers!"

chapter four

THE Marquis raised his eye-brows.

"A caretaker?" he questioned with a hint of laughter in his voice. "That is certainly an unusual occupation for somebody who looks like you!"

As he spoke, his eyes flickered over the gown that Neula was wearing.

He was experienced enough to know that it was very expensive and had doubtless come from Bond Street.

"Mr. and Mrs. Cossins...who were here before... died," Neula explained in a low voice, "and we were... grateful to take the...position and I hope...Your Lordship will let us...stay."

As she spoke she thought frantically that if he sent them away, they had nowhere to go and very little money.

Without thinking, without considering the Marquis's attitude, she said pleadingly:

"Please...let us...stay! We have been very...happy

here and we have cleaned up a great deal of . . . the house which has been . . . completely untended for six months."

Again the Marquis's eyes scrutinised her, and she thought there was a mocking twist of his lips as he said:

"As you appear to know a great deal more about the house than I do, I suggest, Miss Borne, you take me round and introduce me to my property."

Neula's eyes lit up.

"I know you will find it very . . . interesting."

"I am sure you will make it so."

The Marquis was thinking as he spoke and as he looked at her that this was something he had certainly not expected when he arrived at Tremaine Park.

He was sure that Mr. Carstairs had no idea what a strange caretaker was installed in it.

If he had known, he would obviously have mentioned that the caretaker who looked after the Park was not the usual respectable elderly husband-and-wife.

Instead, she was a very glamorous and exceedingly attractive young woman.

The Marquis thought that his exile to the country was certainly going to very different from what he had expected.

As Neula began talking in her soft, educated voice, he knew that he was intrigued by a puzzle which he determined to solve.

If there was one thing the Marquis really enjoyed, it was being confronted by something unusual, and, if possible, a mystery.

He had been well aware that Neula had hesitated before she said her surname, and he immediately suspected it was an invention.

"As you can see, My Lord," Neula was saying, "this is

the Drawing-Room, and I think it is one of the prettiest rooms I have ever seen!"

"I am inclined to agree with you, Miss Borne," the Marquis replied, "but I reserve the right to give preference to my home—Kerne House."

"Which is, I know, in Berkshire," Neula said. "Mr. Ainsworth told me about it."

"What else did he tell you about me?" the Marquis enquired.

He spoke quite casually, and was not prepared for the blush which swept up Neula's face, or the way her eyes looked away from him rather shyly.

Quickly she replied:

"And now I want to show you a room which I am sure you will appreciate even more than this one."

She walked to the door and the Marquis followed her down the passage where the walls were covered with the Tremaine ancestors.

The Marquis, however, made no comment, and Neula opened the door of the large Library.

She knew as she did so that that was because she wanted to read, and had done so every spare moment since they had arrived.

She had insisted on Amy cleaning the Library before they tackled any of the other rooms.

The sun was streaming through the high windows and the velvet curtains had been drawn back.

They were slightly faded, but still were the colour of the roses which Neula was looking forward to seeing later in the formal garden outside the windows.

It suddenly struck her that if the Marquis sent them away, they would lose not only the roof over their heads, but so much beauty besides.

She therefore doubled her efforts to entertain him in his

own house, unaware that her anxiety and fear showed in her very expressive eyes.

They inspected the Library, then the large Dining-Room, where the table could seat twenty people with ease.

There were leaves in the Pantry which could extend the table to hold over thirty.

From there Neula took the Marquis back to the hall.

"There are quite a lot of rooms," she said, "but they are not yet cleaned enough for your Lordship to see them."

"What about the bedrooms?" he enquired.

Neula hesitated, wondering frantically if she could move her mother out of the best rooms without the Marquis being aware of it, then decided to tell the truth.

"You may think it . . . very reprehensible, My . . . Lord," she said in a low voice, "but when we came here everything was covered with dust and we arrived late in the evening."

She glanced at him and went on again:

"It was therefore easier to occupy two of the best bedrooms on the First Floor than to go looking for those which would have been more suitable for our positions, and I am . . . afraid we have . . . stayed in them ever since."

The Marquis's eyes twinkled.

"At least you are honest about it, Miss Borne."

"If you let us stay, we will, of course, move at once," Neula offered.

"I suppose you have left a bed for me?"

"Of course!" Neula answered. "The Master Suite where the General slept is exactly as it was when he occupied it, but we cleaned it as soon as we arrived because—"

She stopped.

She had been about to say:

'My mother felt it only proper that it should look exactly as it had when her father occupied it.'

73

She did not finish the sentence, and as she started to climb the stairs, the Marquis followed her.

By now he had it fixed in his mind that Neula, who he appreciated was very beautiful, had run away reprehensibly.

It would be, he thought, either with a married man or perhaps some scallywag who had no intention of marrying her.

He was wondering what he would say when he met the man in question.

He thought he would be well advised, since his servants would talk, to tell them to find employment elsewhere as quickly as possible.

Then he told himself that if he were truthful, it was a relief to find there was somebody in the house to whom he could talk.

He was sure that if Neula was not too infatuated with the other man, he would enjoy talking to her.

In fact, if he were honest, he thought her very desirable.

He wondered if he would find it a challenge to turn her affections from the man who had brought her here towards himself.

Neula had no idea what the Marquis was thinking, and, intent only on making herself pleasant so that he would allow them to stay, she took him down the passage.

They walked past the State Bedrooms occupied by her mother and herself, and the *Boudoir* in which Louise was resting, to reach the Master Bedroom at the end.

This was a very large room with windows looking south and east.

It was dominated by a huge four-poster hung with red velvet curtains in which the General had always slept.

He had also filled the room with trophies of his life.

There were oil-paintings, most of them rather badly ex-ecuted, of the battles in which he had fought.

His sword hung over the mantelpiece, and beneath it was a long row of his medals in a glass case.

There was also a portrait of him which had been pre-sented by the officers of his Regiment, the Grenadier Guards, when he retired and of which he had always been very proud.

Besides this there were on tables trophies he had won since he had been at School.

There was the Sword of Honour he had been awarded at Sandhurst, and a number of gifts he had received in India from Maharajahs and Princes.

It was quite an extraordinary collection, Neula had thought when she first saw it.

When she saw the surprise on the Marquis's face she gave a little laugh and said:

"General Sir Alexander Tremaine was a very distin-guished soldier!"

"That is obvious," the Marquis replied, "and I think I should feel intimidated if I slept alone in this room!"

He waited after he had spoken.

He was expecting, as had always happened with women in the past, that Neula would look at him provocatively, pretending to be elusive, or with a definite invitation in her eyes.

Instead of which, she answered quite seriously:

"I am sure the General, if he were alive, would approve of your horses and your horsemanship!"

"I cannot believe that you have been reading the racing columns of the newspapers while you have been living here," the Marquis remarked.

"Newspapers here are in rather short supply," Neula answered, not liking to say that she was economising by not having them.

She smiled at him and then went on:

"The whole village was very excited when you won the Steeple-Chase ten days ago at Wimbledon."

"How on earth could you know that?" the Marquis enquired.

Two dimples he had not noticed before appeared in Neula's cheeks.

"You must be aware that ever since you won the house," she said, "everybody on the estate has been insatiably curious about their new owner."

She saw the Marquis was still looking surprised and explained:

"Actually, one of the servants in your house in London is a boy from this village, and your exploits, whatever they may be, lose nothing in the telling!"

If she had wished to intrigue the Marquis, she certainly succeeded, but he merely said a little dryly:

"You surprise me, Miss Neula! And now, before I agree to your suggestion that you stay on here, I think I should meet the gentleman who is here with you."

There was a sarcastic note in his voice as he said the word "gentleman" which made Neula look at him questioningly.

Before she could speak, however, he continued:

"I am imaginative enough to guess that you are in hiding, and, of course, I am hoping you will tell me why, and from whom. I am guessing that you are afraid your father is searching for you."

For a moment Neula was stupefied by what he had said, then the Marquis saw her dimples again.

"If your Lordship will wait a moment," she said, "I will fetch the other caretaker."

She did not wait for him to agree, but ran from the room and into the *Boudoir*, where she knew her mother was resting.

* * *

Louise had in fact slept for a little while.

Now she had risen from the *chaise longue* to tidy her hair in the beautiful oval mirror with its frame of gilded cupids which she remembered had been the delight of her mother.

As Neula put her head round the door, she turned to say:

"I have been very good, darling! I slept for quite a long time, and now I am going to help you with the flowers."

Neula shut the door behind her and said in a breathless little voice:

"Mama! The Marquis is here! Our . . . employer!"

Louise gave a little cry of horror, and Neula added:

"He wants to meet you, and he is in your father's bedroom. Be very careful not to let him know who we are."

"Of course not!" Louise agreed. "At the same time, I suppose we must move out of here. How terrible that he should find us and we had no idea he was coming!"

She was talking as she rose from the dressing-table and walked towards her daughter.

Neula saw that her mother was wearing one of the expensive gowns that Sir Horace had bought for her and looked not only lovely and very fragile, but also obviously a Lady.

She put out her hand and took her mother's in hers, realising as she did so that Louise's fingers were cold.

"It is all right, Mama, do not be frightened!" she said. "Make yourself very charming, or he may send us away with nowhere else to go to."

Louise drew in her breath.

As they walked out of the room hand-in-hand, Neula was saying a prayer that they could stay where they were and not have to start searching for a cottage or lodgings.

The Marquis was standing where she had left him in the General's bedroom.

He was looking at the medals over the mantelpiece and realising what a very distinguished soldier the General had been.

He heard Neula come into the room, and before he turned waited for her to say whom she had with her.

"My Lord, may I present my mother?" Neula asked.

The Marquis turned round.

He had been expecting a man, and Louise, as she dropped him a graceful curtsy, was a complete surprise.

"How do you do, Mrs. Borne," the Marquis said, taking her hand in his. "I had no idea when I came here that my house was being looked after so efficiently by two very charming, if unusual caretakers!"

"We have done a great deal to clean it up," Louise replied, "or, rather, Neula has. I have not been well enough to help her as much as I should."

"I can find no fault with what you have done," the Marquis said, "and my servants, who are on their way down from London, will take the task off your shoulders."

Neula gave a little murmur of horror.

"If your servants are coming . . . I suppose you will have no . . . further use for us and . . . will want us to leave?"

"I have not said so!" the Marquis replied.

"Oh, please," Louise cried, "let us stay! We have been so happy and safe here, and Neula has enjoyed riding your horses."

The Marquis's eyes twinkled.

"I have not yet inspected the stables," he said. "In fact, I had no idea there were any horses here."

"They have been out to grass for nearly a year," Neula said accusingly, "and there was no one to ride them."

"So you made that another of your duties!"

"It may seem to you an impertinence," Neula said, lifting her chin. "But your animals were really neglected, even though they were fed."

"I can understand, Miss Borne, that you have been putting right what was wrong," the Marquis said.

He had a touch of sarcasm in his voice.

"The horses are well-bred, and I think Your Lordship will appreciate them when you have time to see them."

"I am well aware, Miss Borne, that you are taking me to task for neglecting livestock which were certainly my responsibility as well as the house."

Neula gave an exasperated sigh.

"I am not criticising, My Lord. I would not presume to do so."

She pushed out her little chin before continuing:

"I am only explaining why I rode and took care of your horses, who have now been trained so that they can be ridden by anyone . . . even a lady."

The Marquis thought she was quite understandably criticising the women with whom she had been told he associated.

Many of them, it was true, were not good riders, and expected a horse to be perfectly trained before they would dare mount him.

He, however, did not continue the discussion, but said:

"What we have to decide is, when my staff arrive, and you are relieved of your duties, what we should do with you."

Because Neula was proud, she said, holding her head high:

"If we are to leave, My Lord, I hope you will give us time to pack our clothes."

"I am not inhuman, Miss Borne," the Marquis retorted, "and actually I have not said that I wish you to leave."

She looked at him enquiringly, and turning to Louise, he said:

"I have come here alone, Mrs. Borne, because there are reasons why for the moment I wished to leave London."

He paused to smile at her before adding:

"What I am going to suggest is that, since I often find my own company a bore, you stay here in the meantime as my guests."

He saw the excitement on Louise's face as she clasped her hands together.

"Do you . . . really mean . . . that?" she asked.

Then, as if she felt she should not make a decision without her daughter's approval, she turned to look at Neula.

"Perhaps, My Lord," Neula said, "we would not fit in with your friends when they arrive, and they might think we were . . . imposing on . . . you."

"My friends will not be arriving, because I have not for the moment invited any of them to join me," the Marquis answered loftily. "I am therefore appealing to your good nature in asking you to keep me company."

"Are you sure . . . really sure?" Neula asked.

Now her tone was very different and he thought the sunshine was caught in her eyes.

"I seldom say what I do not mean!"

"But surely you do not wish us to occupy your best bedrooms?" Louise enquired.

"I see no reason, as they will be empty if you leave them, why you should not stay where you are."

"Oh, thank you! Thank you!" Louise cried. "I cannot

tell you what a relief it is to know that we can stay here where I—"

She stopped, realising that she had been indiscreet, and gave Neula a quick look of apology, which the Marquis did not miss.

"Now may I suggest," he said, "that Miss Borne show me the stables, and as my staff will not arrive for some time, I would appreciate a cup of tea."

"But of course!" Louise said. "I will make it for you while Neula shows you the horses, and later, if you wish, there are quite a number of bottles of wine left in the cellars, as my fa—"

She stopped again.

She had been about to say:

". . . my father had very good taste in wines," and was relieved when Neula covered up her slip by saying:

"I will take you to the stables, My Lord, and I think you should meet Henry, who is the only gardener left, and who also looks after the horses."

She smiled at him and then went on:

"He is a very able man, and I am sure he would wish to have your assurance that you will continue to employ him."

"I feel sure you know as much about the outside of the house as you do of the inside," the Marquis observed, "so I am prepared to take your advice as to who should be retained or dismissed."

"You must talk to Mr. Ainsworth, the Estate Manager," Neula replied, "and the people in the Home Farm are very kind and very obliging."

She stopped speaking a moment then added:

"Henry will tell them you require milk, butter, and eggs. I expect they can spare you a young lamb, and the farmer known as Jackson also keeps pigs."

"I find your knowledge of my estate most helpful," the Marquis said.

Neula was not quite certain whether he was being sarcastic, or was, in fact, really grateful for any information she could give him.

They walked to the stables.

When the two horses she had trained nuzzled her as soon as she appeared and obviously responded as she patted them, the Marquis had a childish desire to show off.

She had taken the horse named Waterloo out of his stall and into the yard to show him what a well-bred animal he was.

The Marquis, having appreciated how knowledgeable she was, unexpectedly let out a shrill whistle.

There was a pause, then he whistled again, and through the archway which led to the front of the house, Pegasus came hurrying at a sharp trot.

The stirrups were jogging at his sides, his ears were pricked, and he looked, the Marquis thought appreciatively, most impressive.

Neula gave an exclamation of excitement, and as Pegasus stopped beside his owner, he said:

"I feel, Miss Borne, you would like to meet the horse on which I won the Steeple-Chase."

"He is magnificent!" Neula said. "Quite, quite magnificent."

The Marquis was so used to being flattered that he thought it inevitable that she would add: "Like his owner!"

But Neula's eyes were on the stallion.

As she patted his neck and spoke to him in a soft voice the Marquis had the strange feeling that he had been forgotten.

"She is certainly a very unusual caretaker," he said to himself.

He was determined with the zeal of a detective to find out more about her.

*   *   *

Dinner was finished, and the servants left the room.

The Marquis, sitting in the high-backed carved chair in which Louise remembered her father had always sat with an air of authority, said:

"I want to thank you both for making my first dinner at Tremaine Park such an enjoyable one."

"It is we who should be thanking you!" Louise said softly. "I have enjoyed myself more than I have for a very long time."

She thought of Sir Horace as she spoke.

There was a stricken expression in her eyes which made Neula say quickly, in case the Marquis had noticed, which in fact, he had:

"I think your Chef's cooking is superlative! I have never enjoyed such delicious food before, and I much prefer French cuisine to Italian."

"What do you know of Italian food?" the Marquis asked.

Neula realised she had spoken without thinking, then decided there was no harm in telling the truth.

"I was at School in Florence, My Lord," she said, "and as it was a long way to return home I stayed in the holidays sometimes in Italy with some of my friends and also in France."

"And now I suppose you are going to tell me that you speak both languages perfectly!" the Marquis exclaimed.

"I hope I do," Neula answered. "I should be very ashamed of myself if I could not converse fluently in French, Italian, and Spanish."

The Marquis shook his head.

"I am afraid if you are one of those frightening beings known as an 'intelligent woman,' Miss Neula, you will never be a success in Mayfair society!"

Neula laughed.

"I have no wish to be, and at the moment I am very happy here at Tremaine Park."

"You are not to talk like that," Louise said before the Marquis could reply. "You know, darling, I always intended to present you at Court, and arrange for you to have a Season in London."

Neula frowned at her mother, and Louise looked apprehensive as she said:

"I suppose I . . . should not have said that."

"Really, Mrs. Borne, there is no need for you to go on pretending to me, at any rate, that you are ordinary caretakers," the Marquis assured her. "What I am exceedingly curious to know is why you have run away, and from whom?"

He spoke quite lightly and was not prepared for Louise to seem to shrink beside him and say with a note of terror in her voice:

"No . . . no! Please . . . forget what I said. I am so foolish . . . and since we have been here . . . I had . . . forgotten to . . . be afraid . . . and now . . ."

She made a little gesture with her hands that was infinitely pathetic.

Looking at the Marquis pleadingly, she said again:

"Please . . . forget what I said . . . and let us talk about something . . . else!"

Neula rose to her feet.

"I think, Mama," she said, "it would be correct now for us to leave His Lordship to his port, or rather his brandy, and wait for him in the Drawing-Room."

"Yes . . . of course!" Louise agreed.

She moved from the table and slipped her hand into her daughter's.

As the Marquis walked ahead to open the door for them, he saw she was near to tears.

When he went back alone to the top of the table, he told himself he had certainly stumbled onto something very dramatic and interesting.

"I will make Neula tell me what all this is about!" he promised himself.

Finding that he was impatient to talk to her again, he finished his brandy and went towards the Drawing-Room.

He was not surprised, and he told himself it was what he might have expected, to find Neula alone.

"Mama has retired to bed," she explained, "and is very apologetic for being upset at dinner."

The Marquis sat down in a comfortable armchair and waited until Neula, too, had seated herself opposite him before he said:

"You must be aware that I am exceedingly curious!"

"That is understandable," Neula replied, "but there is nothing we can do about it."

"Why not?"

"Because it is a secret. It is best not talked about, and anyway, you should not be involved."

"That is the most infuriating thing I have ever heard!" the Marquis exclaimed. "And I am also extremely hurt."

"Why should you be that?"

"Because you are not trusting me. I have always considered myself a trustworthy person where other people's secrets are concerned."

"When secrets are confided and talked about, they are no longer secrets!"

"There is always an exception to every rule."

"You can hardly expect me to be sure of that when I met you for the first time only this afternoon!"

It was the sort of argumentative conversation which the Marquis greatly enjoyed and which he frequently had with his men-friends.

He persisted in claiming that in the circumstances two women alone should trust him to protect and help them.

Neula's argument was reinforced with quotations from the Classics and from history.

It was that the moment even one person was let into a secret, inevitably it became common property, and in their case would certainly be dangerous.

Because the argument stimulated them both, they talked until Neula realised it was midnight.

"Mama will wonder what has happened to me," she said, "and perhaps she is worrying that because we are not doing what you wanted, you will turn us out."

"Do you always look after your mother in this protective manner?" the Marquis asked. "I should have thought it would be more normal for her to be looking after you!"

"Mama has always had Papa to depend upon and decide everything for her," Neula said after a moment's hesitation, "and now I feel I should take his place."

The Marquis was convinced there was more to it than that, but he did not say so.

As Neula dropped him a little curtsy and held out her hand, she said:

"Goodnight, My Lord, and thank you, more than I can possibly say, for allowing us to stay here with you."

"I should really be thanking you," he replied, "and I would like to express my gratitude in a much more eloquent way than with words."

He did not release her hand, and to Neula's astonishment he put his arm around her and drew her close against him.

She looked up in astonishment and realised he was about to kiss her.

With a little cry of horror she pushed him away, and with a swift movement which took him by surprise, she escaped.

She ran down the length of the Drawing-Room, flung open the door, and went out into the hall without looking back.

The Marquis was astonished.

It was the first time he had ever tried to kiss a woman who had not responded, usually too eagerly.

The ladies in question had, of course, always been sophisticated beauties, very sure of themselves and their attractions.

They expected him to succumb to their allurements, thinking of it as their right.

He thought Neula was very lovely, and while they were arguing he had been sure that her lips, if he touched them, would be very soft, sweet, and innocent.

He was sure, too, they would be very different from the burning, fiery kisses he had exchanged with the Princess.

Now, as he stood alone in the Drawing-Room, he told himself that he had over-rated his own charm.

He had also made what he was sure was a false move where Neula was concerned.

She would certainly be on her guard in the future, and might even consider, if she was really afraid of him, leaving the house.

It was too late now, and the Marquis blamed himself for being very foolish in not realising that Neula, however intelligent she might be, was very young.

He had never had anything to do with young, unmarried girls before.

Now he realised that he had behaved as if she were an older and very much more sophisticated woman who would welcome his advances and reciprocate them.

He knew he had not used his brains where Neula was concerned, and it annoyed him to realise that he should have waited a great deal longer before he tried to kiss her.

He supposed his only excuse was that he had been beguiled not only by her loveliness, which was very different from anything he had found in any other woman, but also by the keenness of her intelligence.

The spirited way in which they had duelled with each other in words had been fascinating, and in several instances she had undoubtedly been the victor.

'It is very different here from anything I expected,' he thought as a little later he went up to bed.

He wondered as he passed Neula's room if she had locked her door.

He thought that because she was so obviously inexperienced where men were concerned, it might never occur to her that he might visit her in her bedroom.

She was certainly chaperoned by her mother, but he had the feeling, and it made him smile, that it was Neula who was doing the chaperoning and directing this strange drama for which he had not yet found an explanation.

"To find it is something I intend to do," he said to himself as his valet left him and he got into the General's bed.

It was very comfortable, and he thought that so far his visit to Tremaine Park had been an unequivocal success.

"Tomorrow I will find out more," he told himself, "and I also have to explore the estate."

There was a smile of satisfaction on his rather hard lips as the Marquis fell asleep.

*　*　*

In her bedroom, Neula, having gone to say goodnight to her mother and finding her almost asleep, thought that the Marquis's behaviour was only what she might have expected.

She remembered what Mr. Ainsworth had said.

What was more, last week the stories that had percolated down from London had been more lurid than usual.

Billy's sister was an excellent embroiderer, as Neula had discovered, who worked at her home for a reputable firm, not in Bond Street, but in one of the shops off it.

She had worked for them before she married and came back to the village, but they had found it hard to replace her.

She therefore both looked after her husband, who worked on one of the farms, and her two children, and at the same time managed to augment the family income by her embroidery.

Last Wednesday she had finished the monograms on some gentlemen's handkerchiefs and had taken them to London, travelling with the Carrier.

He went there once a week to replenish his cart with a multitude of goods which he sold in the local villages.

Having seen her brother as she usually did on her trips to London, she came back with the latest gossip regarding the Marquis.

"Billy says," his sister related to the Grocer and a number of the village women who were shopping, "that 'Is Lordship's in real trouble this time, an' that a Russian Prince be after 'is blood!"

It was only a question of hours before Mr. Ainsworth was told about his employer.

He reported it to Neula when she called on him the following day.

She thought it was polite to let Mr. Ainsworth, who had been so kind to them, know what was going on up at the house.

He was still unable, owing to his accident, to leave the White Cottage.

He was delighted to see her and said:

"Amy tells me that the house looks as it did when the General was alive, and no one can say fairer than that!"

"We are doing our best, Mr. Ainsworth," Neula said, "but there are a great number of rooms that we have not yet tackled."

"There is no hurry," Mr. Ainsworth said, "and I would not want you or your mother to do too much."

"You are so kind," Neula answered, "and we can never be sufficiently grateful to you."

It was then, because he knew she would be interested, that Mr. Ainsworth told her the latest gossip about the Marquis.

She guessed now that this was the reason that he had come to the country.

"I wonder if he is running away from the Princess, or from her husband?" she asked herself.

She then thought it was insulting that because he could not be with the woman he loved he should treat her as a very inadequate substitute.

"How dare he try to kiss me?" she asked. "He is despicable, and just as bad as everybody says he is!"

But, when she got into bed to lie in the darkness, she could not help remembering how handsome he looked sitting at the head of the Dining-Room table.

It had also been fascinating to talk and to argue with him.

"I suppose he is like a 'Pied Piper,' and all the stupid women he meets follow him because they find him mesmeric!" she said disgustedly.

Just before she fell asleep, however, she found herself wondering what it would be like to be kissed, and especially by the Marquis.

The girls at School had talked incessantly about their conquests.

One or two had actually been kissed and described in whispers what it had felt like.

Neula thought it rather embarrassing and had not been particularly interested.

Instead, she told herself stories of a love that was glorious, compelling, and spiritual.

She had the feeling, although she was not certain, that to be kissed by one of the over-ardent dark-eyed Italians or the somewhat supercilious brother of her French friends would not be a rapture.

It would be a humiliation because it was a mockery of real love.

"Mama loved Papa so that she was prepared to run away with him and give up everything—her family and all that was familiar," Neula told herself.

She stopped, and then continued:

"When I love somebody like that, then I shall know that it is real love!"

That the Marquis should want to kiss her on so short an acquaintance was strange enough.

But she had to make him understand that his kisses were something she would never accept, and that it was insulting of him to suggest it.

It put her on a level with the women in London who deceived their husbands and thought that because they loved him, everything that was decent and proper could be forgotten.

She turned over restlessly in her bed before she decided:

"I will make it clear to him tomorrow that if he behaves again in such a way, Mama and I will be forced to leave."

Even as she said the words in her mind she knew with a frightening clarity that they had nowhere to go, and very little money to support them.

She had, before she went up to dress for dinner, taken her money from the safe and hidden it at the back of a drawer in the bedroom.

She had a feeling that the smart, well-paid servants who had arrived from London were better off than she and her mother were, and had more reliable prospects for their future.

"What will we do if I cannot find work?" she wondered.

Then almost as if it were an answer to her question, she saw her father's smiling face and thought she was being needlessly apprehensive.

"You helped me get Mama away from that beastly Sir Horace; you brought us here; and now, Papa," she said, "you have to protect me from the Marquis!"

She had the feeling that her father was telling her not to worry and that everything would be all right.

Then because the idea of it was so comforting, she fell asleep.

chapter five

NEULA awoke early and instantly thought of the Marquis.

She felt it would be embarrassing to see him and wondered how she could avoid doing so at least until later in the day.

Then as she looked at the clock on the mantelpiece she had an idea, and quickly put on her riding-habit and boots.

Having no hat, she arranged her hair as neatly as possible, so that it would not blow about.

Slipping out of her rooms, she went down the backstairs towards the door that led out to the stables.

Although the sun had not yet risen, there were two grooms already brushing down the Marquis's horses, one of which was Pegasus.

She knew, however, it would be a mistake to linger.

She asked the grooms to saddle what she thought of as her own horse and rode away as quickly as she could.

She thought it likely that the Marquis would also want to ride early, but she had no wish to ride with him.

"If I appear to be seeking his company," she told herself, "he will think I am like all those immoral women in London who they talk about in the village."

She took a path through the woods and had a good gallop over the level ground beyond them.

Sometime later she reluctantly turned her horse for home.

Because of her determination not to meet the Marquis, should he be riding early, she chose a route through the Park well away from where she thought he was likely to ride.

She then made her way round the back of the copse which was just beyond the bridge spanning the lake.

She was walking her horse slowly, thinking of how exciting it had been the night before until the Marquis had spoilt it.

Then she was suddenly aware there was a horse amongst the trees.

She could see the swish of its tail, and wondered if perhaps one of the horses had escaped from the paddocks.

Then she realised that the horse was being ridden and she was curious as to who the intruder might be.

It was most unusual to find a stranger riding in the Park, for the men and boys from the village always came on foot.

She decided to ask him what he wanted, and turning her horse's head, she moved towards the trees.

Although she was still a little distance from them, she could not see the rider clearly and realised he was a gentleman, and well-dressed.

She drew nearer, and as she did so, he turned to look at the bridge on the other side of the wood.

He bent forward to do so and as he moved, Neula saw something glitter in his right hand.

To her astonishment, she realised that it was a pistol.

Instinctively she drew her horse to a standstill.

Then, as the man straightened himself in the saddle, she thought there was something strange about the shape of his head and the angle of his tall hat, which did not look at all English.

Suddenly she knew who he was.

Moving slowly so that he would not be alerted by the sound, she waited until she was out of sight, then galloped back to the stables as quickly as she could.

As she gave her horse to a groom, she asked:

"Has His Lordship gone riding?"

"Nay, Miss, but us be a-takin' Pegasus round t'the front door in a few minutes."

Neula ran into the house.

She was breathless by the time she reached the hall where there were two footmen in attendance.

"Is His Lordship down yet?" she asked.

"No, Miss," one of them replied, "but 'Is Lordship's breakfast be ready for him when 'e comes."

Neula said nothing.

She went back the way she had come and opened a door near the Pantry.

It led into the Gun-Room, where her Grandfather's guns and all his other sporting equipment were kept.

They were still exactly where he had left them when he died.

Several shot-guns and two rifles were on one side of the room in a cabinet with glass doors.

On the other wall were hanging salmon and trout rods, gaffs, and landing nets.

Neula had not yet inspected the room thoroughly, but she knew there was a glass-covered table in the centre of it, where she saw what she was seeking.

Carefully arranged in the case were the pistols the General had used on military service.

Several of them were old models which were now obsolete, but one was of a much later date.

There were two duelling-pistols and some very ancient weapons which must have belonged to his ancestors.

There was also a small pistol which looked like a miniature of the others.

Neula knew from what her mother had told her that the General used to carry it in his pocket in dangerous countries when he was in evening-dress.

She opened the lid of the table and took out first the most up-to-date of the service-pistols.

She loaded it with bullets which she found in a drawer under the table.

Then after a moment's hesitation she put the small one, after she had loaded it from the same drawer, into the pocket of her riding-jacket.

She hurried back to the hall, and without her asking, the footman to whom she had spoken before said:

"'Is Lordship's down, Miss, an' gone into t'Breakfast-Room."

Neula went down the passage to the room that had always been used for breakfast because it faced the morning sun.

It was smaller and less formal than the Dining-Room.

The Marquis, as she expected, was sitting at the head of the table.

He had a newspaper propped up in front of him on a silver stand which he was reading while he ate.

He glanced up as Neula entered the room, and without waiting for him to greet her, she said:

"You are in danger, My Lord, and I have brought you a pistol with which to protect yourself!"

The Marquis stared at her in surprise.

"What do you mean—in danger?" he enquired.

Neula sat down in a chair beside him, putting the pistol she was carrying down on the table between them.

"I was coming back from my ride," she explained, "when in the copse just beyond the bridge I saw a man on a horse."

She paused a moment, then dropped her voice as she went on:

"He was looking towards the house as if he were waiting for somebody to appear, and he had a pistol in his hand!"

"Are you sure?" the Marquis asked. "It seems extraordinary if it is true."

"He was riding a well-groomed horse and was smartly dressed."

She stopped speaking, and then continued slowly:

"Even at a distance I could see that there was something un-English about him, and I think, My Lord, it is the Prince!"

Now the Marquis's expression of surprise turned into one of sheer astonishment.

"What do you mean—the Prince?" he asked sharply.

"Prince Kluchusky," Neula said as if she thought he was being very dense.

The Marquis stared at her.

"How in the world, living here, can you know anything about Prince Kluchusky?"

For the first time, because she had been so intent on saving him from what she was sure was the Prince's plan to kill or at least to injure him, Neula felt embarrassed.

Her eyes looked down and there was a faint flush on her cheeks as she said:

"I was told . . . that the Prince was very . . . incensed with Your . . . Lordship . . . "

"Who told you that?" the Marquis demanded.

Neula thought she should not involve Mr. Ainsworth, so she replied:

"Everybody is . . . talking about it in the . . . village."

"I find this very hard to believe," the Marquis said. "Are you sure you are not imagining that it *is* the Prince, and that he actually has a pistol in his hand?"

"You can go and look for yourself," Neula answered, "but as he is hiding among the trees, I imagine he intends to take you by surprise and ride away before anybody sees him."

The Marquis's lips tightened and he said beneath his breath:

"How the devil could he know that I was here?"

Neula had no answer to this and she sat looking at him wide-eyed with a look of fear on her face.

She had read enough about Russia and the Russians to know that they were easily aroused to tempestuous passions.

Also she knew that the sanctity of life meant very little to them.

She was quite sure in her mind that Prince Kluchusky thought that he had been insulted.

He thought his honour was at stake, and was waiting to take a murderous revenge on the Marquis.

As if he could read her thoughts, the Marquis said:

"Very well, I will come to see if this is just a figment of

your imagination or is actually, which I think very unlikely, happening."

He got up from the breakfast-table as he spoke, and Neula, picking up the pistol, held it out to him.

He looked at it, then he said:

"No!"

"You are not taking it with you?"

"No!" the Marquis said again. "The Prince, if he is really there, will be too much of a gentleman to shoot an unarmed man, and I have been expressly forbidden to duel with him!"

Reluctantly, Neula put the pistol down on the table, and as the Marquis reached the door, he said:

"You had better come with me and show me where he is. I suppose if you could approach him without his being aware of it, I can do the same."

Neula thought this was intelligent of him, and as the Marquis collected his hat and whip, she had a sudden idea.

"I think it would be wise if you gave the order for Pegasus to be taken back to his stall," she said, "and we left the house by another exit."

The Marquis was quick-witted enough to realise she was telling him that the Prince, if he was in the wood, could see the front-door from where he was waiting.

He would therefore think it strange that the Marquis, once mounted, did not proceed immediately over the bridge, as he would normally have done.

He thought for a moment before he said:

"I have a better idea!"

He turned to one of the footmen and said:

"Tell the groom holding Pegasus to stay where he is outside the front-door, and that I will be there in a few minutes."

"Very good, M'Lord," the footman replied, and ran to do his bidding.

The Marquis looked at Neula, and she went ahead to show him the way to the door she had used once already that morning.

It led to the stables from the side of the house.

Once they were there the Marquis gave a sharp order for two horses to be saddled for them.

Within a few minutes Neula was leading him down the back of the stable-yard and through the paddock into an open field.

At the end of this there was a stream that fed the lake.

It was quite small and shallow, and there was a point where it was easy to cross without the horses getting more than their fetlocks wet.

Then she rode ahead towards the place in the wood where she had seen the Prince.

She felt her heart beating faster and knew it was because she was afraid, first that the Prince would not still be there, which would convince the Marquis that she had imagined it.

Secondly, if he was there, there would be a bitter scene between the two men over the Princess Natalia.

She thought it would be embarrassing, and also somewhat degrading, that she should be present when the Prince accused the Marquis, as the village gossipers believed he had, of seducing his wife.

"If they start quarrelling, I shall ride away," Neula told herself.

Slowing her pace down to a walk, she moved forward to the place in the field from which she had seen the Prince's horse amongst the trees.

He was still there, leaning forward as when she first saw him.

He was obviously watching the house and expecting to see the Marquis come through the front-door and mount Pegasus.

The Marquis drew a little nearer until he was close enough to the Prince to say without raising his voice:

"Is Your Highness waiting for me?"

The Prince started and turned round in the saddle.

Neula saw she had been right in thinking he was holding a pistol in his right hand.

For a second he just stared at the Marquis, then he turned his horse round to face him, saying as he did so:

"Yes, My Lord, I was waiting for you, to inform you that I am taking the Princess back to Russia. But before I go, I intend to teach you a lesson!"

"If you mean by making use of that offensive weapon you hold in your hand, may I inform you that I am un-armed?"

He paused a second and then went on:

"And while I am quite prepared for you to call me out in the traditional fashion, I am unfortunately handicapped by His Majesty's express command that there will be no duelling between us."

"I am aware of that," Prince Kluchusky replied, "but that does not deter me from avenging myself, as I intend to do."

He snarled the words.

Neula thought apprehensively that there was a look in his eyes which, combined with his high cheek-bones and dark hair, gave him the ferocious appearance of a wild beast.

"I think," the Marquis said, almost drawling the words, "that it would be more civilised if we talked about this over a glass of wine."

The Marquis stopped speaking, and indicated with his hand as he went on:

"I therefore suggest that Your Highness accept my invitation to come with me to the house."

"If you think I would soil my feet by walking into any house that belonged to you, you are very much mistaken!" the Prince said. "I have had a detective following you, and what he has reported to me makes me determined to kill you!"

"And face the hangman for doing so?" the Marquis asked contemptuously.

The Prince made an angry sound.

"You forget I have Diplomatic Immunity and therefore cannot be brought to trial in your Courts of Law!"

He paused before he went on:

"All you can do now, Kerne, is to say your prayers, and remember you have received your just deserts!"

He raised his arm as he spoke preparatory to bringing down his pistol at the Marquis, and Neula knew he would aim at his heart.

With a swiftness that sprang from a sense of urgency activated by sheer fear that the Marquis would die, she pulled the small pistol from her jacket-pocket.

Her bullet struck him a split-second before his pistol was on target.

Although she prevented him from shooting the Marquis in the heart and killing him, the bullet, in fact, passed through the sleeve of the Marquis's riding-coat exactly the same height at which it would have struck his heart.

Then as the Prince's pistol clattered to the ground, the horses of both the men reared and bolted.

The Marquis managed after a few lengths in the open to bring his horse under control.

The Prince's horse dashed through the trees and a low branch swept his rider from the saddle.

He lay sprawled on the ground, the blood pouring from his wrist.

Neula's horse was older and less nervous and had not galloped away.

It moved restlessly but under control.

She looked down at the Prince with a pale face and frightened eyes.

The Marquis came riding back to her.

"Thank you, Neula," he said in a quiet, steady voice. "Come, I will take you home."

She was perturbed to see that blood was soaking through the sleeve of his riding-coat and said:

"You must have . . . your arm seen to . . . at once! What . . . about . . . the Prince?"

"Forget him!" the Marquis replied. "I will send somebody to attend to him, but I expect he has servants somewhere in the vicinity!"

He spoke casually, as if it were not of the least importance.

Because Neula found it difficult to speak, she followed him as he forded the stream and hurried up the incline which led to the stables.

When they reached the stableyard, his left arm was hanging limply at his side and blood was now dripping from his cuff.

A groom helped him from the saddle and he walked in a commendably steady way into the house followed by Neula.

When he reached the hall he said in the authoritative manner in which he always gave orders:

"Send Tomkins to me immediately!"

He then started to climb the stairs, but had reached only the second stair before he staggered.

Neula, speaking for the first time since they had left the wood, said to the footmen:

"Help His Lordship upstairs!"

Two of them did as they were told, while a third ran ahead to find the Marquis's valet.

Neula watched the Marquis's progress until he reached the landing.

Then to her relief she saw the Butler come hurrying from the direction of the Pantry.

"What's happened, Miss?" he asked.

"His Lordship has been injured," Neula replied. "Send a groom as quickly as possible for the doctor! Anyone in the village will know where he lives."

She paused, then she added:

"Tell the groom outside that Pegasus will not be required this morning."

Then she ran upstairs to her mother's room.

Louise was horrified on hearing what had occurred.

"How can you have been so quick, darling, in saving the Marquis's life?" she asked.

Neula suddenly, to her surprise, felt a little weak and sat down in a chair.

"It was Papa who . . . taught me to shoot," she answered rather shakily. "He said . . . one never knew when it . . . might come in . . . useful."

Louise fetched her a glass of water and as she sipped it, Neula went on:

"I never thought the Marquis would be so . . . fool-hardy as to . . . face the Prince without a . . . weapon in his hand, with which to . . . defend himself."

"I can understand his reasoning," Louise replied. "No

gentleman would shoot at an unarmed man, and it is horrifying that the Prince should be so uncivilised."

"He is Russian, Mama," Neula said, "and he was . . . defending his honour!"

"You should not know about such things!" Louise answered.

Neula did not speak.

She was lying back with her eyes closed, thinking it was very fortunate that she had not killed the Prince.

She had aimed for his hand, but by hitting his wrist she had saved the Marquis, which was all that mattered.

She found herself wondering what she would have felt if it had been the Marquis whom she had seen lying on the ground.

Supposing he had been shot through the heart, as the Prince had intended, or at least unconscious?

It would have been like seeing one of the great oak trees struck down, she told herself.

She knew, too, it would have been a tragedy if he had died in such an ignominious manner, indeed if he had died at all.

"He is so interesting . . . and at the same time so vital and so . . . compelling," she told herself.

Then she remembered she had thought of him as the "Pied Piper."

She was ashamed at the thought that if she was not careful she would be another of the foolish women who followed wherever he led.

* * *

The Doctor arrived within the hour, and when he came from the Master Bedroom, Neula was waiting to speak to him.

He was quite a young man who had come to the village only recently, so that her mother had never heard of him.

"Will you tell me how His Lordship is?" Neula asked. "My mother and I are staying here as his guests and we are naturally very anxious."

"I understand from what His Lordship told me," the Doctor said, "that he was shot at by some lunatic, doubtless a poacher, in the woods."

Neula thought that was the type of explanation the Marquis would make, and she nodded her head in agreement, as the Doctor continued:

"His Lordship has lost a lot of blood, but it is only a flesh wound and I have given him something to take away the pain and make him sleep."

He looked at Neula in a critical manner before he went on:

"His valet tells me that he can nurse him quite competently, but I am sure it would be a help if you could assist him in any way. There is no chance of my getting a nurse, even if I sent to London."

Neula knew this was true, and she felt the Doctor, although he did not say so, was apprehensive at leaving the Marquis entirely in the hands of servants.

"Both my mother and I," she said, "have had some experience of nursing, and, of course, we will do our best for His Lordship."

"I am sure that would be a great help," the Doctor replied. "I will call again this evening, but in the meantime I do not think you will have any trouble."

He went down the stairs and Neula went to the Master Bedroom and knocked on the door.

It was opened by Tomkins, a spry little man who, she had learned from the other servants, had been with the Marquis for many years.

The previous evening the maid called Rose, who looked after Neula, had said, when she was helping her dress for dinner:

"We've come 'ere at such speed, Miss, that I don't know if I'm on me 'ead or me 'eels!"

Neula had laughed and Rose went on:

"It's all very well for Mr. Tomkins, His Lordship's valet! 'E's bin with 'im for over ten years, an' 'e's used t'these ups and downs!"

She paused and looked stern as she went on:

"I'm not, an' Mrs. Meadowfield, the Housekeeper, 'as retired to bed with a sick-'eadache!"

Neula had sympathised with the woman, and she guessed now as she saw Tomkins that he was as efficient as he looked.

"I have just seen the Doctor," she said, "and I have told him that both my mother and I are used to nursing, and we are very willing to help you with His Lordship."

She thought as she spoke how often they had been obliged to bandage her father when one of the horses he was breaking in had thrown him.

Sometimes he was only bruised, but at others bleeding, or with a strained muscle.

The same had applied to a stable-boy they employed who, as Louise often said, was remarkably "accident prone" and was always in some trouble or another.

"That's real kind of you, Miss!" Tomkins exclaimed. "An' it'd be a great 'elp if yer would sit with 'Is Lordship for a short time while I goes and gets the bandages I packed when we comes down from London."

"Of course I will," Neula agreed.

She went into the Master Bedroom as Tomkins hurried away.

The blinds were half-drawn to keep out the glow of the

sun, and the Marquis, lying in the great velvet-curtained bed, was asleep.

Neula sat down and looked at him.

Her first thought was that he looked very handsome, then that he looked younger and somehow different from his appearance yesterday and this morning.

She realised it was because he was quiet and still.

He was therefore not so overwhelming and authoritative or so magnetic.

It made her know that she was no longer afraid of him, in fact, that she no longer hated him as she had when he had tried to kiss her.

Now he looked just like a rather spoilt child who had always had his own way regardless of other people's feelings.

"He is clever . . . very clever . . . and he has been . . . kind to us," Neula reasoned.

She also thought it was brave, although foolhardy, of him to have confronted the Prince without any means of defending himself.

She could see the top of his bandaged arm and realised he was naked under the sheets.

It did not seem shocking. Indeed, for the moment, she was no more embarrassed by him than she had been by Ben the stable-boy.

Ben had cried against her shoulder after breaking his collarbone and she and her mother had undressed him.

'I suppose all men are like little boys when they are hurt,' she thought.

She wondered if one day she would have a son whom she would look after and protect.

She hoped if she did, he would be as handsome as the Marquis.

Then abruptly she told herself that these were rather

foolish thoughts and she should find something better to do.

There was a bookcase in the room.

She pulled out a volume at random and found it was a novel by Sir Walter Scott.

It was a story she had read before and was only too willing to read again.

Yet, when she started, instead of being utterly absorbed, as she was usually, her eyes kept rising from the printed page to look at the Marquis.

He was very quiet, but she thought he was paler than he had been at first, and attributed it to his loss of blood.

'He will soon be well again,' she thought, 'and wanting to ride.'

He had said yesterday at dinner that he intended to visit all the farms one by one, and he expected her to show him the way.

Neula knew that by consulting her mother she could find out where they all were.

She had therefore said eagerly that it was what she would like to do, and she was sure the farmers would be delighted to see him.

"Like everybody else on the estate, they are very curious about you!" she said.

Now she knew not only that she was disappointed, but so would the farmers be when he did not appear.

She supposed it might be at least a week before he was well enough to ride.

'At least we are needed here, and will not be sent away,' Neula thought triumphantly.

It was then that she was shocked by a thought that came unbidden into her mind.

It was that perhaps if the Marquis had kissed her last night, it might have been very wonderful.

Louise came slowly down the stairs after having sat with the Marquis, who was a little feverish, while Neula went riding.

Tomkins, who had been up all night, had gone to his room to rest, and now Neula had taken her place beside the bed.

"It is such a lovely day, Mama," she said, "and I think you ought to go out in the fresh air, or else I shall have two invalids on my hands!"

"You are spoiling me," Louise replied, "but I assure you I am so much better that soon I shall give up all this nonsense of resting and being treated like a child."

Neula kissed her.

"Do not argue, Mama, just do as I say. The sunshine will do you good."

Louise had therefore put on a pretty bonnet which was almost too smart for the country, but which made her look very attractive.

She was intending to obey her daughter's orders, when she heard the sound of wheels outside the front door, and somebody came up the steps.

She paused, wondering if it was the Doctor, although he had already been earlier that day.

Then as a footman went to the door a voice said:

"I wish to see the Marquis of Kerne!"

"I'm sorry, Sir, but he's not at home," the footman replied respectfully.

"I find that hard to believe!" was the reply. "Will you tell him the Earl of Grantham is here to see him!"

Knowing the footman was going to find it difficult to convince the caller that the Marquis could see no-one, Louise hurried down the last steps of the stairs.

Going to the front door, she said:

"I am sorry, but His Lordship is not allowed visitors at the moment."

Then, as she looked up into the face of the man standing facing her, she gave a little gasp.

He stared at her incredulously before he exclaimed:

"Louise! It *is* Louise?"

"Yes, of course! Oh, David, it is such a surprise to see you!"

"What are you doing here of all places?"

She hesitated, then, aware that the footmen were listening, she said:

"Will you come in?"

The Earl obeyed her, and handing his hat to one of the footmen, followed Louise into the Drawing-Room.

As the door shut behind them he said:

"I think I must be dreaming. I have often thought of you and what you were doing. Then, of all unlikely places, I find you in your own home!"

Louise took off her bonnet as if she felt constricted by it as she said:

"I have a lot to explain, and what has—brought you here?"

"It is not really surprising, considering that I live only five miles away!"

"But the house has been empty for some time."

"Yes, of course I know that," he replied, "but I was told this morning by Dr. Gibson that the Marquis was here and there is something I want to discuss with him."

He was talking as if what he was saying did not hold the whole of his attention, for his eyes were on Louise.

As she sat down on the sofa she looked very lovely.

Her hair was golden against the blue cushions and her

111

eyes, raised to his, held an expression he did not understand.

"You look exactly as you did when I last saw you!" he exclaimed.

"I wish that were true," Louise smiled, "but I am numerous years older!"

"And so am I," the Earl remarked, "but you are still the loveliest person I have ever seen in my whole life!"

"But you have changed your name!"

"I came into the title very unexpectedly, for there were three lives between me and it, two years after you ran away with Charles."

"I had no . . . idea of it."

"The only thing I could think about was that if it had happened earlier, and I was no longer only a penniless second son with no prospects, perhaps I would have had a chance, Louise, of winning you."

Louise looked at him in surprise.

"Did you really . . . feel like . . . that about . . . me?"

"Of course I did! You must have been aware of it."

"I had no . . . idea!"

"I loved you, I think, from the first moment I ever saw you."

He paused a moment, to smile at her, then continued:

"You must have been seven at the time, and quite the most beautiful child I could ever imagine, like a small angel!"

Louise laughed.

"Oh, David, you are very poetical!"

"That is what I have always been where you are concerned, and later I wrote poem after poem to you."

"But you never gave them to me!"

"How could I? I had nothing to offer you then, and

when I might have been brave enough, you had eyes only for Charles."

He gave a deep sigh before he went on:

"But how could I have imagined, how could I have guessed for one moment that you would run away with him when I was well aware that neither of you had a penny to bless yourselves with?"

"I know," Louise said softly, "but we were very happy, so happy, David, that I have wished almost . . . every day since I . . . lost him that I could have . . . died too."

The Earl's fingers tightened on hers, then he said:

"Tell me why you are here, and what has happened to Sir Horace Harlow?"

Louise gave a frightened cry.

"How do you . . . know about . . . him? Who . . . told you?"

"I was away when Charles died," the Earl explained, "but as soon as I came back I called to see you."

He gave a sigh and continued:

"I learned from an old man in the garden of the empty house that you and your daughter had gone away with Sir Horace Harlow the day before I arrived, and that you intended to marry him!"

Louise looked away.

"Y-yes . . . I married him!" she said in a dull voice.

"Then what has happened? Is he here with you?"

"No . . . no . . . but, David, you must not . . . tell anybody . . . especially the Marquis . . . that I am Lady . . . Harlow. They know me here as . . . Mrs. Borne!"

"But why?"

Louise hesitated for a moment, then she said:

"When my daughter Neula came back from School in

Florence . . . she found . . . Sir Horace was being very . . . unkind to me . . . and we . . . ran away!"

"What do you mean—he was unkind to you?" the Earl asked sharply.

Louise did not answer, and he said:

"Tell me, Louise! I have a right to know!"

"H-he was very . . . angry because he thought when I married . . . him that I would . . . give him the s-son he wanted. He had however . . . when he was young . . . contracted a fever in Africa which . . . prevented him . . ."

Louise's voice trailed away, and the Earl said:

"Black Water Fever! I have heard of it and how it affects those who suffer from it. But surely Sir Horace understood that in the circumstances it was not your fault."

"H-he began to . . . hate me," Louise said, "and . . . Neula thought I was not . . . strong enough to . . . stand any . . . more."

The words seemed to come like a whisper from between her teeth.

"Are you saying," the Earl asked incredulously, "that he struck you?"

Louise nodded.

"My God!" he exclaimed. "How could that happen to you of all people?"

He looked at her with horror on his face.

"If I had known, I would have killed him and taken you away, but as it was, how could I interfere?"

"If only I had . . . known!" Louise said miserably. "I knew it was . . . wrong when I loved Charles so much, to marry anybody else, but I had to . . . think of Neula . . . and we had no money!"

"No money?"

"None, either then or now. Which is why we came here as caretakers."

The Earl stared at her.

"I do not believe it!"

"It is true! Then when the Marquis arrived... unexpectedly, he was... very kind and said we could... stay on as his... guests."

"I find myself bewildered by what you are telling me," the Earl said. "But the only thing that matters is that I have found you, Louise, and now I will never let you go!"

His voice dropped as he said:

"Oh, my darling, I have loved you all my life, and I have never been able to look at another woman."

Louise tried to take her hand from his.

"You must not... talk like that. I... I am... married I ... am... married to Sir Horace... and Neula would be very... shocked... if she knew what you were saying."

"If it is true that you have no money and are hiding from Sir Horace, then I think, Louise, you will find me useful, for at least I can provide for you in the future."

He was silent for a moment. Then he said:

"Do you think Sir Horace would divorce you?"

Louise gave a little cry of horror.

"How can you think of anything so scandalous? If Horace knows where he can find me... he will compel me to... go back and... I could not... face it all... over again!"

There were tears in her eyes and the Earl said:

"I swear to you that is something you will never do! I am here, my precious, and I will not allow you to be unhappy."

He stopped speaking to look at her closely, then added:

"So smile at me and tell me, even if you still love Charles, that I have a small place in your heart."

He waited until Louise raised her tear-filled eyes to his.

"Quite a . . . large place! Oh, David . . . it is so . . . wonderful to find you again when I . . . have known . . . you all my . . . life!"

chapter six

NEULA had just reached the top of the stairs from the hall, when she saw a footman carrying the Marquis's breakfast-tray away from his bedroom.

He was followed by two housemaids staggering under a pile of sheets and pillow-cases which had been changed on his bed.

Following them came the Housekeeper, walking stiffly in her black silk gown, her chatelaine dangling from her waist.

It always amused Neula to see the enormous number of people whom the Marquis employed to contribute to his comfort.

She knew it delighted her mother to see that the house was being run almost exactly as it had been in her father's day.

As she walked along the corridor towards the Master Bedroom, Tomkins came out.

"'Mornin', Miss!" he said cheerily. "'Is Lordship's jus' like 'is old self, sittin' up in bed, givin' orders!"

Neula laughed.

"I will go and listen to him," she said, "and you must have a rest. You have had hardly any sleep these last three nights."

"It wasn't too bad last night," Tomkins said, "and thanks very much, Miss, for 'elpin' me."

He walked away before Neula could say any more, and she knew he was always embarrassed when she praised him.

No one could have looked after the Marquis more efficiently.

He had run a high fever and, if not delirious, was very restless during the night.

Neula and Louise sat with him in the daytime, but Neula was aware that the Earl of Grantham was waiting downstairs and her mother was a different person since he had appeared.

Louise enjoyed talking over old times with him, and Neula did not have to be told that he loved her mother in the same way that her father had.

'If only Mama were free,' she thought wistfully.

She opened the door of the Marquis's bedroom and found the sunshine pouring its golden rays into the room.

She walked towards the bed, saying as she did so:

"Tomkins tells me you have had a good night. I am so glad."

"I feel like myself again," the Marquis said, "and I intend to get up!"

Neula gave a little cry.

"It is much too soon! You must have the Doctor's permission first!"

The Marquis smiled.

"Are you still bullying me, Neula? I seem to remember your forcing some very unpleasant medicine down my throat and commanding me to sleep when I wanted to stay awake!"

"It was all for your own good."

"That is what my Nurse used to say, and I found then, as I have always found since, that what is 'for my own good' is invariably unpleasant!"

Neula sat down on a chair facing him and she said in a different tone of voice:

"I expect you want to hear what has . . . happened to . . . the Prince."

"I am hoping that you hurt him considerably more than he hurt me!" the Marquis remarked.

"Dr. Gibson told me that he was in great pain, but is considering leaving tomorrow, the Inn at Potters Bar, where he has been staying."

The Marquis did not speak and Neula said in a frightened voice:

"You . . . do not think . . . you do not imagine that he will . . . try again?"

"It is unlikely," the Marquis replied, "but if he does, I am sure you will somehow manage to save me."

He looked at Neula, then held out his hand, palm upwards.

Almost as if he were hypnotising her, she slowly put her hand in his.

As she felt his fingers close over hers, there was a faint flush in her cheeks.

She looked away from the Marquis as he said quietly:

"I have not yet thanked you, Neula, for saving my life, it was very brave of you."

"I . . . think we must be wise and forget it," Neula said hesitatingly. "Dr. Gibson told me that the Prince said he had been attacked by a Highwayman."

She stopped speaking and smiled at him, then added:

"That could also be the . . . explanation for . . . your wounds."

"I am not interested in what the Prince thinks or says, but in you!" the Marquis said. "I have never known a woman who was so 'quick on the draw,' or such a good shot!"

"Papa taught me, thinking it might be useful."

"It was certainly useful to me!" the Marquis remarked dryly. "And now I have to think of how I can thank you."

Neula remembered how he had tried to thank her before, and she looked away, the colour deepening in her cheeks.

She would have taken her hand away from the Marquis's, but he held tightly on to it.

"Have you forgiven me for the way I behaved the first night after we dined together?"

Neula did not answer and he went on:

"I am very contrite, and was very much ashamed of myself after you ran away. My only excuse is that you looked so enchantingly lovely that I forgot how young you were."

Still Neula could find nothing to say and, although she gave a little tug of her hand, the Marquis held it firmly in his.

"Now," he said, "I want to tell you what I feel about you and, as words are inadequate, it would be much easier to thank you in kisses!"

"N-no . . . of course you . . . cannot do that!" Neula said quickly.

"Why not?" the Marquis enquired.

She felt his eyes were on her lips, and with a quick movement he did not expect, she managed to release her hand from his.

"If you are thinking of running away," he said, "I shall get out of bed and follow you!"

Neula, who had been rising from her chair, sat down again.

"You are blackmailing me," she accused him, "and it is very unsporting!"

"You know the answer to that," the Marquis replied. "'All is fair in love and . . .'"

"If you cannot talk of anything sensible," Neula interrupted, "I shall go away! And if you follow me, as you threatened to do, your arm will start bleeding again."

The Marquis laughed.

"What I like about you, Neula," he said, "is that you never say what I expect you to. But I want to talk to you and I will be 'sensible,' as you call it."

"And I have something quite exciting to tell you first," Neula interrupted.

"What is it?" the Marquis enquired.

"The Earl of Grantham called to see you two days ago, and he turned out to be a very old friend of Mama's, whom she knew when she was a child."

She paused a moment and then went on:

"He comes every day to talk to her about old times while he is waiting to see you."

"I know what he wants," the Marquis observed. "He talked to me about it when we were in London."

Neula waited, a question in her eyes as he explained:

"He has some very well-bred mares that he wants sired

by Pegasus and some of my other stallions. It will be quite easy to arrange it while I am here."

There was a little pause before Neula said hesitatingly:

"H-how long will you . . . be staying?"

"Does it matter?" the Marquis parried.

"It . . . it is just that . . . if you expect Mama and me to leave . . . when you do . . . we shall have to look for other accommodation."

"I know that would alarm you, and perhaps it is something you cannot afford," the Marquis said quietly.

Neula looked at him in astonishment.

"H-how do you know that? I have never . . . said so."

"I am using my brain, and perhaps I am more perceptive than you credit me with being," the Marquis replied. "Meanwhile I am still waiting for you to trust me with your secret."

Neula clasped her hands together.

"Please, do not prove . . . and try to find out things we do not want to . . . tell you," she begged. "It will only make everything more . . . difficult than it is . . . already, and will upset . . . Mama."

"When you talk like that," the Marquis replied, "there is nothing I can do."

He stopped to smile at her, and then said:

"At the same time, Neula, I think it is extremely unkind that, having saved my life and nursed me back to health, you still treat me as if I were a stranger."

"I . . . I do not do that! I promise you . . . I do not do that!" Neula said.

She spoke with a passionate sincerity.

Then as she looked at the Marquis her eyes were held by his.

It seemed as if it were impossible to look away, and he was telling her something she did not understand.

122

Louise had promised to take her turn at looking after the Marquis while Neula went riding before luncheon.

When she knew her mother would soon be coming along the corridor, Neula said in a low voice:

"Please . . . do not upset Mama. She is happier at the moment than she had been for a long time."

She smiled at him and went on:

"If you start . . . cross-examining her and letting her know how . . . curious you are about us . . . she will be upset all over again."

"Why should you imagine I would do anything so unkind?" the Marquis asked angrily.

"I am only . . . warning you."

"You have made what you are thinking very plain," he said. "I will try in future to be indifferent to your concerns and interested only in my own."

Neula gave a little cry.

"Now you are making me feel I have been rude and ungrateful. Please . . . do not take umbrage over what I have said."

Her eyes were pleading as she said:

"I want to tell you . . . I promise you I do! But it is not my secret . . . and we so much want to stay here, where no one knows . . . who we are."

She thought as she spoke that it was dangerous enough that the Earl knew the truth.

But as he was in love with her mother, she knew he would do everything to make her happy and prevent Sir Horace from finding her.

But Neula had a presentiment that the comfort and luxury in which they were living was only a dream.

Sooner or later they would wake up to reality to find

themselves once again running away frantically to hide from Sir Horace.

'Mama is his wife, and he has the law on his side,' she thought miserably.

She had no idea that all her anxiety and foreboding was very obvious to the Marquis.

Once again he put out his hand to take hers.

He felt her fingers flutter in his like a small bird, and he knew strangely, but as positively as if somebody had told him so, that he was in love.

Never before had he felt so protective, so concerned about any woman.

He knew that what he wanted was to put his arms around Neula and tell her that he would look after her, and that nobody would ever frighten her again.

His feelings were so intense but so unusual that he questioned them, and thought perhaps they were part of his fever.

He looked at Neula sitting beside him with the sunlight bringing out the red in her hair.

He knew she was not only more beautiful than anyone he had ever seen before, but she appealed to him in such a different way.

He had known this from the first moment he had seen her, but had not realised it was love.

Always before, all that love had meant to him was a fiery exchange of passion such as he had had with the Princess.

They had enjoyed each other entirely physically and with a sensual fierceness.

He recognised that he had found in Neula something spiritual and so exquisite that what he felt for her came from his heart.

It was something else in his make-up which he had not thought about since he was a young boy.

He supposed those who were religious would call it his soul, but to him it was a craving for something coming from the infinite and beyond anything earthly or mundane.

He had been aware of it when he had seen something of great beauty, or heard it in the sound of great music.

Looking back into the past, he could remember he had felt it when his mother's arms were around him and she had taught him his prayers.

Now this strange, unaccountable rapturous feeling was what he felt for Neula.

At the same time, he enjoyed simply talking to her, and being stimulated by the originality of her thoughts.

He enjoyed the way in which she tried to defeat him in arguments on subjects which had nothing to do with their relationship as persons.

And yet, he thought, even that first evening when they had matched their wits at the Dining-Room table, he had been pulsatingly aware that she was different.

So very different from anybody he had ever known before.

He had a desire to tell her what he was feeling, but was afraid of frightening her away from him as he had done when he had tried to kiss her.

The Marquis was very intelligent, and he had exercised self-control, when it was necessary, all his life.

As he held Neula's hand in his and looked into her eyes, he told himself that he would win her love if it took him his whole lifetime to do so.

He knew, however, he would have to be very careful.

She would be on her guard because of the stories she had heard about him, which, he thought a little wryly, were none of them to his advantage.

Louise came into the bedroom looking as lovely as her daughter and, as the Marquis realised at once, very much happier than he had ever seen her before.

She bade him good-morning, then said to Neula:

"Your horse is waiting for you outside the front door, so hurry and change, dearest. It will be good for you to get out into the sunshine."

"I will leave the Marquis in your hands, Mama," Neula said, rising from the chair in which she had been sitting, "but you will have to be very strict with him if he talks of getting up!"

She went from the room as she spoke and ran down the passage to change into her riding-habit.

"Is there anything I can get you?" Louise asked.

The Marquis shook his head.

"Sit down and tell me about David Grantham. Your daughter tells me that you knew him in the past."

Louise looked shy and he went on:

"I had forgotten he lived near here, but now it makes me wonder if perhaps your home was in the neighbourhood."

"I . . . I do not want to talk about . . . myself," Louise replied, "but David is very eager to see you. Do you think you will be well enough to talk to him this afternoon?"

"I am sure I shall," the Marquis replied.

He was thinking as he spoke that perhaps the Earl would furnish the next clue in the puzzle he was trying to unravel.

What was the reason Louise and Neula had run away?

* * *

The Earl arrived just before luncheon and Louise, who was downstairs in the Drawing-Room, said apologetically to Neula, who had just joined her:

"I asked David to luncheon . . . I hope it does not matter?"

"No, of course not!" Neula replied. "Did you tell His Lordship?"

"I suppose I should have done, but as he was beginning to ask me questions about David, I was so afraid I would say something indiscreet and he would guess why we were here."

"Oh, do be careful, Mama!" Neula pleaded. "It would be a disaster for anybody to know the truth."

"Except for David . . . we can trust David?"

She looked so worried as she asked the question that Neula said quickly:

"Yes, of course, Mama. But tell him to be very careful what he says when the Marquis interrogates him, as I am sure he will."

* * *

Dr. Gibson arrived during the afternoon and after he had left Neula went to the Marquis's bedroom.

"I have won!" he announced as soon as she appeared. "Tomorrow your jurisdiction over me as an invalid comes to an end!"

He smiled at her before continuing:

"I am allowed to get up, and as it is something I intended to do anyway, I am glad to have what you must accept as 'professional approval.'"

He spoke defiantly and Neula replied:

"I was thinking only of you. Are you quite certain your arm is well enough?"

"I can answer that by telling you that I shall be riding again by the end of the week!" the Marquis retorted, and his voice was quite stern as he added:

"In the meantime, I have had a Chess board brought

upstairs, and I will challenge you to a game, warning you as I do so that I often play at my Club."

"That tells me you are taking an unfair advantage!" Neula protested.

She sat down beside the bed, eagerly remembering how she had played Chess with her father and though he was a skilful player, she had sometimes beaten him.

She hoped now that even if she could not prove her superiority over the Marquis, she would at least make it a good fight.

They played and talked, and Neula managed to make it a very close finish before the Marquis was able to make the final winning move.

She had enjoyed the game all the more because she was hoping he would not notice that Louise had stayed downstairs.

This was because the Earl had not left after luncheon.

He had walked round the garden with her mother, then announced that he was staying for tea.

Neula had left them alone.

She knew she was not wanted and was aware that nothing could be better than to hear her mother laugh as she used to do before her father's death.

At the same time, she could not help worrying what would be the outcome of it all.

Not only was Louise's happiness to be thought about, but also the Earl's.

She was afraid that sooner or later his relatives and friends would ask themselves why he was continually visiting Tremaine Park, and if there was some other attraction there besides the Marquis.

"You are looking worried!" the Marquis said after their game was finished.

He bent forward and said very gently:

"Let me help you! I know you need help, and I am quite intelligent when it comes to problems and difficulties."

"I am sure you are," Neula said, "but . . . you know I cannot talk about it . . . so stop trying to tempt me into doing something which . . . I must not do!"

"You are making me frustrated and very cross!" the Marquis said.

Neula started to reply, then got up and walked across to the window.

The sun was sinking behind the huge oak-trees in the Park in a blaze of golden glory.

The loveliness of it made her draw in her breath.

She thought with so much beauty to look at, the Marquis to talk to, and the comfort of her grandfather's house, she would be the happiest person in the world.

If only she did not have to worry about her mother and Sir Horace.

Then she heard the Marquis say in the same exasperated and cross tone he had used before:

"Damnit! You are enough to try the patience of a Saint!"

Because it was so unexpected for him to speak in such a manner, Neula felt the tears fill her eyes.

She hung on to the window-sill to prevent herself from running back to the bed and pleading with the Marquis not to be incensed with her.

His voice had pierced her mind and, she thought, her heart, almost as if he had driven a dagger into her.

Then as she fought against the pain of it and her tears blotted out the sunshine, she knew that she loved him.

How was it possible for her not to love him, when he was so handsome and at the same time so kind and understanding.

She tried to remind herself of all the scandal she had heard about him.

How shocked it had made the people in the village, Mr. Ainsworth and herself, when they repeated what they knew of his love-affairs and the women who followed him, as they said, like a "Pied Piper."

"How can I be so foolish, so idiotic, as to love a man who, when he leaves here, will never think of me again?" she asked herself.

Then as she stood with her back to him she heard him say in a very different tone:

"Come back to me, Neula! I am sorry if I sounded cross. It is just that I cannot bear to know you are unhappy and to see the fear in your eyes."

There was something beguiling, gentle, and also so mesmeric about the way he spoke.

Neula wiped her eyes like a child with the back of her hand and walked slowly back towards the bed.

As she stood beside the bed looking at him, he put out both his hands and without thinking she gave him hers.

He pulled her forward so that she sat down on the side of the mattress.

A little shyly her eyes met his, and he could see the marks of her tears.

They looked at each other for a long moment, until, as if the words seemed to burst from the Marquis's lips, he said:

"I have hurt you, and that is the last thing I meant to do! Oh, my darling, you must know by this time that I love you!"

Neula could only stare at him incredulously.

"I did not mean to tell you," he went on, "and I will not be a nuisance or worry you until you love me."

His fingers tightened on hers until the pain of it made Neula realise that what she was hearing was real and not just a figment of her imagination.

But she had to be sure.

"D-did you say . . . that you . . . l-love me?" she asked in a hesitating voice.

"Of course I love you!" the Marquis declared. "I feel as if you have been part of me for years and that we have known each other over centuries of time rather than just a few days!"

He drew in his breath before he continued:

"Perhaps that is true! I have been searching for you all my life. I have known you in other lives, and now I have found you again."

He stopped speaking to smile at her, before adding:

"You are everything I have always looked for and wanted in a woman, and thought it impossible to find."

"It . . . it is not . . . true!" Neula whispered. "You . . . cannot be . . . saying this to me!"

"But I am saying it!" the Marquis said. "Do you imagine that even when I was running a high fever these last days I was not aware of your presence in this room?"

He spoke with an intensity that made every word seem different from anything he had ever said before.

As Neula just stared at him, her eyes seeming to fill her whole face, he said with a twist of his lips:

"I told myself that I would be very controlled and not try to win you until we had known each other for much longer."

He paused a moment, then continued:

"But my love is too overwhelming to be constrained any longer, and I can only beg of you, my darling, to try to understand what I am feeling for the first time in my life."

He raised one of her hands to his lips.

As he kissed the softness of her skin and she felt as if the kiss burnt its way into her heart, Neula felt the tears run down her cheeks.

"You are crying!" the Marquis said. "My sweet, my precious, what have I said? What have I done to make you cry?"

"It...it...is because I am so...happy!" Neula sobbed. "It had been so frightening trying to...look after Mama...all alone...and being terrified...in case...we were found and now...you love me!"

"I love you!" the Marquis confirmed.

Very gently he pulled her closer to him.

As his arms went round her, her head fell back against his shoulder, and he was cradling her in his arms as if she were a child.

He looked down at her, at her eyes seeking his, and at the tears on her cheeks.

Her lips were trembling not with fear, but with sensations which he felt seeping through him at the same time.

Then he drew in his breath and slowly, as if he forced himself not to act quickly, his lips came down on hers.

It was a very gentle kiss as he tried to remember that she had never been kissed before.

To Neula it was as if the gates of Paradise had opened and he took her into a radiance of light that seemed to come from him and to be within herself.

It filled the whole room and the world outside.

She felt his arms tighten and hold her closer still, and yet she was not afraid.

She knew only that this was the love she had wanted to find and thought could never be hers.

It was the love she sensed her father and mother felt together.

It was so glorious and ecstatic that she knew what she was feeling was beyond her imagining, beyond her dreams.

Only when the Marquis raised his head did she say in a rapt little voice which was little above a whisper:

"I . . . I love you! I love . . . you!"

"And I love you!" the Marquis said. "How can you make me feel like this? How is it possible that I have never known what love really meant until now?"

He did not wait for her reply, but was kissing her again.

Kissing her until there was nothing but an ecstasy which made them no longer human but part of Heaven itself.

* * *

Neula left the Marquis's room before dinner.

She felt as if she were walking on clouds of glory and it would be very difficult to come down to earth again.

When she went to look for Louise she found to her consternation that her mother was in her bedroom crying.

"Mama! What is the matter?" she asked.

"Oh . . . dearest . . . I am so . . . unhappy!"

"But . . . why?"

"Because I feel I should not . . . stay here to . . . spoil David's l-life!"

"Why should you spoil his life?" Neula asked.

For a moment her mother did not answer. Then she said:

"H-he loves me! He has loved me all my life . . . and he wants me to . . . go away with him!"

"Go away with him?"

"He wants to . . . take me abroad, to Paris or Italy, where we can live . . . together and . . . no one will . . . ask questions."

Neula sat down on the sofa on which her mother was lying and said:

"B-but surely . . . Mama, you should not . . . do that?"

"Of course I shall do . . . nothing of the sort . . . it is

wrong . . . wicked," Louise said, "since I am m-married to somebody . . . else."

She paused and gave a deep sigh before continuing:

"But how can I live the rest of my life as I am now . . . spoiling your chances of having . . . any friends and making David so . . . unhappy because he says he will never love anybody . . . but me?"

Neula thought it would be a mistake to tell her mother what she felt for the Marquis at this particular moment.

It might drive her into going away with the Earl simply so as not to spoil her daughter's chances of marrying a man she loved.

It suddenly came to her mind that if, which she wanted more than anything else in the world, she married the Marquis, then Sir Horace would know where to find her mother.

He would undoubtedly make things extremely unpleasant.

How could she allow her mother to return to Sir Horace, knowing how he would treat her?

At the same time, that meant that as long as they were in hiding, she would not be able to marry the Marquis.

The idea of her mother going away to live openly in sin with the Earl was horrifying and, she was quite certain, wrong for them both.

Her mother was too sensitive, too sweet-natured, too conventional at heart ever to endure living a life of deceit.

Neula had heard, when she was in Florence, of people who had left England, having deserted a husband or a wife, to live with someone else.

Inevitably, sooner or later, their pretence of being married and the false name they assumed became known.

Then they were ostracised by everybody except others who were behaving immorally like themselves.

'Mama could never live like that,' Neula thought despairingly.

She said aloud:

"Do not upset yourself, Mama. You have looked so happy and pretty lately because the Earl was with you, and I am sure he would not want you to be so distraught."

"He says it is because I am living an . . . impossible life that he . . . wishes to take me away and look after me," Louise said in a broken voice. "But . . . would that make it any better?"

She paused a moment and then went on:

"And I am sure, my dearest, it would not be the . . . right life for you."

"It would not be the right sort of life for you either, Mama," Neula said.

"Then what can we do? Oh, Neula . . . what can . . . we do?" Louise asked.

Then she was crying again; crying pitiably but, Neula thought, quite differently from the way she had cried when Sir Horace had struck her.

She realised that while her mother would perhaps never love anybody in the same way that she had loved Charles, she undoubtedly already had a deep affection for David Grantham.

This would grow with the years into a deep and lasting love and make them both very happy.

Yet Neula was sure that what the Earl was suggesting would ultimately destroy her mother.

For the moment she did not want to think about herself.

She realised that if it became known that she and the Marquis were in love, it would bring disaster upon them in the shape of Sir Horace.

She put her arms round the sobbing Louise and held her close to her, asking despairingly in her heart:

"Oh, God, what can we do? Help us . . . please . . . help us!"

*　　*　　*

The next morning Louise stayed in bed with swollen eyes and a headache and Neula felt almost as unwell herself.

She forced herself to get up, and because she knew there was no reason to sit with the Marquis after breakfast now that he was so much better, she went riding.

For the first time she found no enjoyment in riding one of his magnificent horses.

Instead, she felt her problems besetting her to the point where she could think of nothing else.

She rode across the Park, galloped down the long straight, then came back behind the copse in which she had seen the Prince lying in wait to attack the Marquis.

She thought once again of how it had swept over her that the Prince would have shot and probably killed the Marquis had she not intervened.

She thought now that perhaps it was love, although she had not been aware of it at the time, for the most striking, handsome man she had ever seen in her life that had made her act quickly enough to save him.

Now she had to tell him, and she thought it was foolish that she had not realised it before, that they could not be married.

As soon as it became known that she and her mother were staying at Tremaine Park, they would have to go away in order to escape from Sir Horace.

"But . . . where to? Where can we go?" she asked despairingly.

She longed, although she knew it was impossible, to leave everything in the Marquis's hands.

Confronted by problems that were far too difficult for

her to solve, she felt very young, very inexperienced, and perhaps foolish.

And yet she knew it would be a mistake to involve the Marquis.

She felt that he, like the Earl and all other men, would think the world well lost for love.

Then eventually they would come to regret anything which caused a scandal or was in any way detrimental to their dignity and their family honour.

"Mama and I must go away," Neula told herself.

She thought of how little money they had and knew it would be almost impossible, if they took all their luggage with them, to get away from Tremaine Park without the Marquis and Earl being aware of it.

They would certainly try to dissuade them, and the Earl would renew his pleading to Louise to go abroad with him.

'It would be wrong . . . wrong!' Neula thought.

Then she wondered if anything could be worse than hiding in some obscure place, always tormented by the fear that they would be discovered by Sir Horace.

Without the protection of the Marquis and the Earl, how could they refuse to do whatever Sir Horace demanded.

Neula was sure he would insist that her mother return to him.

He would be too proud, too afraid of scandal and censure, to admit openly that she had left him.

She was sure now that he was searching for them surreptitiously.

Perhaps he was pretending that his wife had just gone away for a holiday and would be shortly returning home.

Neula rode on until her horse was tired and she was exhausted not through riding, but with thinking and coming to no conclusion.

Then, as she rode home, she told herself the one thing

she must not do was to upset her mother any more than she was at the moment.

"Until I have planned it all out in my mind, I must appear cheerful and confident that everything will come right," Neula decided.

Then every nerve in her body cried out that loving the Marquis as she did, she longed to stay with him.

To leave him would be like losing one of her limbs.

She arrived back at the house shortly before luncheon.

When she had quickly changed her riding-habit for a gown, she came downstairs in search of her mother and met the Earl coming in through the front door.

"Good morning, Neula!" he said.

She took him by the hand, and leading him across the hall into the Writing-Room which they had never used, she said:

"I want to speak to you."

He smiled and she thought how charming he was.

"Of course," he said, "it is about your mother."

"She is very upset."

"Upset? I thought she seemed happy when I left her."

"After she had thought over what you suggested, she knew it was very wrong."

"Of course it is wrong," the Earl agreed, "but do you think it is right that you should both be hiding here under an assumed name? You cannot live like this for ever."

"That is what I have asked myself," Neula said, "but, please do not press Mama to go away with you."

She shook her head, and then added:

"She would not be strong enough to stand up to that sort of existence and she would always feel she had ruined your life."

"She almost ruined my life nearly twenty years ago

when I loved and lost her," the Earl said quietly, "and I cannot, Neula, lose her again!"

"I know what you are feeling," Neula said, "but, please, do not let us hurry. Let us think it out very carefully."

The Earl smiled.

"You are very sensible, but far too young to have to cope with such an impossible situation. You were very brave in taking your mother away from that fiend who was ill-treating her."

He stopped for a moment and then added:

"Now somehow we have to make sure she is happy in the future."

"That is what I want," Neula said. "But, please, do not be in a hurry."

"I will try not to be."

He put his hand on Neula's shoulder as he said:

"I know your mother is also thinking of you. This is not the right sort of life for you to be leading."

He smiled at her, then went on:

"I will do everything I can to see that you are looked after by one of my relations."

Neula knew what he was going to suggest, and she said quickly:

"You are very kind, but, please, for the moment just make Mama happy and do not make her distressed as she was last night."

They went together into the Drawing-Room and there was no need for Neula to say any more because Louise was waiting for them.

Although she was obviously pleased when she saw the Earl, there were lines round her eyes that had not been there the previous day and she was very pale.

The Earl kissed her hands, one after the other, as he said:

"We are going to spend a very happy afternoon together, and I have brought my Phaeton so that I can take you driving round the estate."

"I would like that," Louise said in a rather pathetic little voice, and the Earl kissed her hand again.

They were waiting for luncheon to be announced, when the door opened and the Marquis came in.

Neula and Louise both gave a cry of surprise as he walked across the room looking very much like his usual self.

He was, however, being careful how he moved his left arm.

"I have been waiting to see you, Drogo," the Earl said, holding out his hand, "but I did not expect you to be down so soon!"

"I am perfectly all right now!" the Marquis said firmly. "And tired of being molly-coddled and bullied by two beautiful, if domineering, nurses!"

The Earl laughed.

"You are a very lucky man, and I am not going to listen to any complaints!"

The servants brought in wine glasses and a bottle of champagne in an ice-bucket.

The Earl drank to the Marquis's health.

"I have a toast of my own," the Marquis said after thanking them, "and that is to a very clever, very lovely young lady who is responsible for my being here at this moment!"

He raised his glass to Neula as he spoke, and when the Earl looked puzzled, the Marquis said:

"It is a secret, but perhaps we can tell David about it some time!"

"Oh, yes, please let us do that!" Louise begged. "I have

been longing to tell him, but Neula said no one else was to know."

"If I am being left out of this family party," the Earl said, "I shall be very upset."

"I can understand your feelings!" the Marquis said. "There is nothing more frustrating than being kept in the dark!"

He looked pointedly at Neula as he spoke.

Then as she looked back at him a little defiantly, their eyes met and suddenly they were alone, and there was no one else in the world.

Everything was forgotten except their love which seemed to envelop them like a rainbow.

chapter seven

AFTER luncheon was over they sat talking until Neula exclaimed:

"I am sure Tomkins wanted you to rest this afternoon. You must not do too much on your first day."

"I am resting while I talk to you," the Marquis protested, "and actually my arm is practically healed and I feel extremely fit."

They had related to David the whole story of the Prince and his murderous attempt and he had been horrified at the Russian's behaviour.

He had also been astonished that Neula had been both astute and skilful enough to save the Marquis.

"How could you have been so foolhardy to trust a man like the Prince not to shoot you down in cold blood?" he asked him.

"Quite frankly," the Marquis replied honestly, "I had forgotten how uncivilised some Russians can be."

He gave a sneer and added:

"I never imagined that any man would behave so dishonourably, especially when a Lady was present."

"He might have shot at you, dearest!" Louise exclaimed in horror. "And that is . . . something I could not have . . . borne!"

She spoke with such feeling in her voice that the Earl instinctively put out his hand to take hers.

The Marquis watched them with a twinkling of his eyes and to Neula the Earl's love for her mother was very obvious.

She felt a little embarrassed and was sure the Marquis, supposing Louise to be a widow, would ask for an explanation why they would not be married.

She said hastily:

"I am sure you should go to rest, My Lord, then perhaps you will be able to come down to dinner tonight."

Even as she spoke she decided that later in the day she must tell her mother that they must go away.

It was something she dreaded doing.

At the same time, she was convinced it was the only possible solution.

She was confident that her mother would also realise it was what they must do.

Once again she asked herself how she could leave the Marquis.

She knew that it would be like tearing herself in two to deny her love when it seemed to flow through her like the sunshine.

She could no more stop it than prevent the world from turning.

Looking at him sitting back in his high-back chair, relaxed and very much at his ease, she thought that no man could be so handsome or have a more compelling personality.

'Perhaps I am just being absurd like all those other women who have loved him,' she thought, 'and he will quickly tire of me, and go back to his gay life in London and forget me.'

She wondered if what she would feel then would be comparable to what she was feeling now, having decided she must creep away without his being aware of it.

She must make sure that not only Sir Horace could not find them, but neither could he.

While the others were talking she was planning that she and her mother would leave very early the next morning before the Earl was called.

They could then be well away before he realised what had happened.

"I must pack all Mama's things as well as my own tonight," Neula decided, "and as soon as it is dawn, I will send the night-footman to the stables to order a carriage and horses."

She knew the footman would think it strange, but he would not query an order she gave him, and the same applied to the grooms in the stables.

They would drive to the nearest Posting Inn and send the Marquis's carriage home while they continued their journey.

What she had to decide, and decide quickly, was where they should go.

She thought there must be a great number of small villages where, if they could find a cottage, it would be impossible for the Marquis to find them.

Just as it had been impossible, because they had changed horses and carriage so many times, for Sir Horace to discover where her mother had gone, so it must be this time.

She was turning over her plan in her mind, trying to make sure there were no flaws in it, when she was aware that the Marquis was watching her.

She forced herself to smile at him.

"You are very silent, Neula!" he said.

"I was concentrating on what Mama and the Earl were saying," Neula said quickly, and knew that the Marquis did not believe her.

"I am going to take Louise into the garden," the Earl said, looking towards the French windows and the garden.

Rising to his feet, he went on:

"She needs some sunshine on her cheeks, in fact, I have never seen her look so pale."

Neula knew it was because her mother had cried so piteously the night before.

Louise, however, managed to say with a little touch of spirit:

"Are you insinuating that I am looking plain?"

"That would be impossible!" the Earl answered gallantly.

There was a soft, caressing note in his voice as he spoke, and without thinking, Louise put out her hand towards him.

As she did so, the door opened and the Butler announced in a voice that sounded like the trumpet of doom:

"Sir Horace Harlow, M'Lord!"

Neula and her mother seemed to freeze into immobility as Sir Horace came into the room.

He was looking even larger and more menacing, Neula thought, than when she had last seen him.

His face was crimson, his nose turned bulbous by his drinking.

As he moved blusteringly towards them, Neula was aware that he must have already drunk a great deal that day before he arrived.

He walked within a few feet of Louise, who was standing as if paralysed by his sudden appearance, her eyes dark with fear, her lips trembling.

"So here you are!" Sir Horace roared in a voice that seemed to fill the whole room.

He scowled viciously at her as he continued:

"A nice dance you've led me! It has cost me a pretty penny to put two Bow Street Runners on your track!"

"I . . . I was . . . forced to go . . . away!" Louise faltered.

Her voice was so faint that it was hard to hear it.

"Forced?" Sir Horace shouted. "You mean that damned daughter of yours persuaded you to leave me! Well, I'll deal with her as I will deal with you, when I get you home!"

"I . . . I am not coming back . . . with you, H-Horace," Louise answered. "Y-you made me very . . . unhappy and now that I am back in my old home . . . I realise it is impossible for me to . . . live with you . . . again!"

It was a brave speech for Louise to make.

As if he understood that this was a battle in which he must not be engaged, the Earl moved away for her to stand beside the Marquis's chair.

"You are my wife!" Sir Horace shouted. "You will come back with me, and I will prevent you very forcibly from doing anything like this again!"

There was something so menacing in the way he spoke that Louise instinctively took a step backward as if she were afraid that Sir Horace might hit her.

It was then that Neula moved towards him.

"You have to listen to what Mama is saying, Sir Hor-

146

ace," she said, her voice steady although she felt very frightened.

She took a deep breath and went on:

"You were making her ill, so ill that I will not allow her to be made so unhappy or knocked about so brutally ever again."

"*You* will not allow?" Sir Horace almost shrieked. "Who are you to interfere, you penniless chit who stole away my wife and my money!"

His face was growing more and more flushed as he said:

"You will obey me and stop setting my wife against me, or I will beat you into submission, as I intend to beat her!"

"You will do nothing of the sort!" Neula retorted angrily.

As she spoke she stepped in front of her mother as if to protect her.

The Marquis had been watching and listening intently, but thought it best to say nothing yet.

"Curse you! Do not dare to defy me!" Sir Horace thundered. "You are coming back with me now, this minute, and I will have no more nonsense from either of you!"

He raised his arm as he spoke, as if to strike Neula and knock her out of the way.

But as the Marquis now jumped to his feet to intervene, Sir Horace's arm seemed to be suspended in the air above his head.

His whole face was suddenly convulsed, making him look even more grotesque.

He gasped as if for breath, staggered unsteadily, then with a guttural cry that seemed to be forced from between his lips, he fell forward with a crash onto the carpet.

For a moment Neula could not move, or even breathe.

Then as Louise gave a little cry of horror, the Earl's

arms were round her and he carried her out through the French doors into the garden.

The Marquis walked to where Sir Horace was lying and bent over him for a few seconds.

Without speaking, he put his arm round Neula and led her to the door.

She was so shocked, so horrified at what had happened, she did not realise what he was doing until they were out in the hall.

The Marquis shut the door firmly behind him.

Then, still with his arm around Neula in case she should collapse, he said to the Butler:

"Send for Tomkins immediately! The gentleman who just called has been taken ill, and he will know what to do."

"Very good, M'Lord."

The Butler sent a footman hurrying up the stairs and the Marquis drew Neula down the passage towards the Study.

They had almost reached it before she was able to ask weakly:

"Mama?"

"David will look after her," the Marquis answered, "and I will not have you any further upset."

"H-has he . . . had a . . . stroke?" Neula managed to ask.

"He is dead!" the Marquis said. "I imagine it was a heart-attack and he was no longer breathing."

"Is that . . . really true?"

"I am sure of it," the Marquis replied. "Even if he does linger, it will not be for long."

"Then we will . . . not have . . . to go . . . away?"

It was the first thought that came into her mind.

The Marquis put his arm round her and held her close against him.

"Do you really think I would have let you? I knew what

you were planning, and had every intention of preventing you or your mother from leaving the house."

"You . . . knew?" Neula asked in surprise.

"I can read your thoughts," the Marquis said, "and I know the secret you have kept hidden from me."

He smiled at her before he went on:

"I can now understand why you took your mother away from that drunken brute, and brought her back to her own home."

Neula's eyes stared at him in amazement.

"You . . . know that . . . too?"

"It was not very difficult," the Marquis said. "Your mother more than once gave away that she had been here before, and there is a striking resemblance to you both in many of the portraits of your ancestors."

"I was . . . so certain it would be a . . . mistake for you to know why we . . . were in hiding," Neula said weakly.

"It certainly gave me a great deal to think about," the Marquis replied.

He pulled Neula down onto the sofa beside him and she put her head on his shoulder with a little sigh of relief.

"Now we can tell you everything, and why we came here as your Caretakers."

"It is a position in which you are going to remain!" the Marquis said.

She looked up at him, not understanding, and he said:

"You have captured my heart and now you have to take care of it for the rest of our lives."

"Do you . . . really . . . mean that?"

The Marquis's answer was to kiss her, and it was a long time later when Neula managed to say:

"Do you think Mama is all right?"

"I am quite certain we can leave your mother's well-being to David's care," the Marquis said. "I have often wondered why he never married and now I know the answer!"

"He wanted to take Mama away . . . but I thought it was wrong for her to do . . . what he wanted."

"I imagine from what you say that he asked her to go abroad with him, but you were prepared to prevent it."

"Perhaps it was presumptuous of me," Neula said humbly, "but I knew Mama could never stand up to the . . . sort of life in which she would be sneered at and . . . ostracised by other women."

"And now that problem does not arise," the Marquis said. "Your mother can marry David Grantham, and they will be very happy together, just as we shall be."

Neula did not answer and after a moment he said very tenderly:

"Do you really think that I could live without you? And that this is just a passing phase in . . . my life?"

"How did you know . . . that was . . . what I was . . . thinking?"

"Not only are your eyes very expressive, but we are linked together in a strange manner," the Marquis answered, "which is inexplicable, but very real."

He drew nearer as he said:

"You belong to me, Neula, as I belong to you! Even the Marriage Ceremony cannot make us any closer than are our hearts and our souls already!"

Neula stared at him in surprise.

She had never expected the Marquis, of all people, to say anything like that.

But she knew what he was saying was true, and it was what she felt herself.

She loved him until he filled the sky, her whole world, and there was no one else except him.

Then he said very softly:

"That is what I think too. How can I have been so lucky, my darling, as to have found you in, of all strange places, a house I had completely forgotten I owned until I was forced to leave London."

"We felt so safe because you . . . never came . . . here."

"Now I am thinking that it is a very good thing I did, since you have been looking for me as I have been looking for you for a very long time."

He did not wait for her answer, but kissed her until they felt as if the walls were whirling round them, and there was no ceiling overhead.

Only a sky brilliant with sunshine as he carried her once again into the Paradise he had given her before.

"I love you . . . I love you!" she whispered when he raised his head.

Then as the door opened they moved apart and Tomkins came in.

"I thought you ought to know, M'Lord," he said, "that the gent'man's dead! I've 'ad him taken to the Doctor in his own carriage."

"That is what I hoped you would arrange, Tomkins," the Marquis replied. "I suppose there was nothing you could do for him?"

"Nothin', M'Lord. The Doctor'll confirm what I knows already, that 'is 'eart 'ad given out, an' no one could've saved 'im."

"Thank you, Tomkins, you have been very helpful."

"As I knows this 'as bin a shock, M'Lord," Tomkins said, "I've taken the liberty of orderin' a bottle o'champagne for Your Lordship, and I thinks as 'ow Miss Borne should've a glass as well!"

The Marquis smiled.

Tomkins opened the door a little wider and a footman

came in bearing a bottle of champagne and some glasses on a tray.

He set it down on a side-table, and when they were alone Neula said:

"I do not really . . . need champagne. I am so happy . . . so thrilled that Mama need no longer be afraid, and that she can forget she ever married anyone so . . . horrible as . . . Sir Horace!"

"I think David will see to that," the Marquis answered, "just as I am going to see that you think only of me, and of nobody else."

He was speaking with a teasing note in his voice but Neula replied in a tone of deep sincerity:

"I do that . . . already."

*　　*　　*

It was the Marquis who arranged everything.

He enjoyed, as Neula knew, the organisation of two weddings which must be kept very quiet, and a secret for the time being from the outside world.

"What we have to do first, David," he said when the Earl and Louise came back from the garden, "is to get two Special Marriage Licences from the Archbishop of Canterbury."

"Two?" Louise exclaimed.

Then as she understood she ran towards Neula and kissed her.

"Oh, dearest, are you really going to marry the Marquis? I am so glad! I have liked him more and more every moment we have been here, and I know he will look after you."

"I myself have already promised to do that," the Earl said, "but if Drogo is prepared to take on the responsibility, of course I will withdraw my claim to be a very kindly Stepfather!"

It flashed through the minds of them all that nobody could have been a worse one than Sir Horace.

"Neula and I are going to be very happy," the Marquis said quickly, "and all we have to do now is to make certain that there is no scandal or gossip about any of us."

Louise looked worried.

"Perhaps . . . Neula and I should . . . go away . . . somewhere and live . . . quietly until it is correct and . . . proper for us to be . . . married."

The Earl laughed.

"Do you really think I would let you do that?" he asked. "We are being married at once, however unconventional it may be."

He gave her a loving look before adding:

"Never again do I want to see you look so unhappy as you looked this morning—like a flower that had been left out in the rain!"

Louise gave him a little smile and the Marquis said firmly:

"There is no argument about what we should or should not do! We are going to be married here in the Chapel at the back of the house."

He paused a moment and then went on:

"I understand it has not been used for many years, so no one will suspect that a service is taking place there."

Neula drew in her breath, and the Marquis went on:

"I will send for my private Chaplain at Kerne to perform the ceremonies, after which, I think, David, you should take your wife to Venice or somewhere equally romantic for your honeymoon."

As he spoke, Louise smiled and held on to the Earl's arm.

"Neula and I," the Marquis went on, "will be sailing down the coast in my yacht to Cornwall, where I have a house which I have not visited for a very long time, and which belonged to my mother."

He looked at Neula as he spoke, who said very softly:

"It sounds very . . . exciting!"

"It will . . . be," the Marquis promised.

He was, as Neula had told him, a born organiser, and it was only two days later that his private Chaplain arrived from Kerne.

An hour later David and Louise were married with nobody else in the Chapel except the Marquis and Neula.

It was a very moving Service because the Chaplain, an elderly man, made every word seem meaningful.

When he blessed them, Neula felt her father was beside her, giving his approval, knowing better than anybody else that it was impossible for Louise to live alone, with nobody to look after her.

"She will be very happy," Neula told herself, "and although she will not feel the same glory and magic as she felt with Papa, and as I feel with the Marquis, she will be content."

She could not help adding to herself:

"And perhaps gradually she will come to love David as much as he loves her."

*   *   *

After the Service was over, it was time for luncheon.

Because Louise looked so happy and the Earl was like a man who had found the Holy Grail, it was, Neula thought, a meal they would always remember.

When the servants had left the room, the Marquis toasted the bride and bridegroom and said:

"Everything has been done in such a hurry that we have had no time to buy you a wedding-present, which is an important item on these occasions."

"You are not to think of anything so unnecessary," Louise said quickly. "You were so kind in letting us stay here when you found us sleeping in the best bedrooms, and behaving as no proper Caretakers should!"

"I sometimes wake up in the night," the Marquis replied, "and think that instead of coming here, I might have gone to one of my other houses!"

He gave a chuckle as he went on:

"But then I would never have found Neula and acquired a Caretaker who can never give in her notice!"

They all laughed at this, and he went on:

"Because I am so grateful, I therefore intend to give you, Louise and David, as a wedding-present—Tremaine Park!"

For a moment Louise could hardly believe what she had heard, then as she gave a cry of sheer happiness the Earl said:

"That is very generous of you, Drogo. As you are aware, as a result of the fire I had two years ago, half of my own house, which was never as impressive as this anyway, was burnt down."

He made a very expressive gesture as he added:

"So I have no words to say how grateful I am to have the correct background for Louise."

"I thought that was how you would see it," the Marquis said complacently.

As she had no words with which to thank him, Neula slipped her hand into his.

* * *

When Louise and David had driven away on the first stage of their journey across France, Neula and the Marquis were married in the Chapel.

Just as she had felt her father's presence earlier, Neula was sure that he was now giving her away, as he would have done had he been alive.

She also felt the Chapel was not empty.

It was filled with a Heavenly Choir whose voices seemed to vibrate within herself and the Marquis and become a paean of happiness rising up to the sky.

As he put the ring on her finger and they knelt hand-in-hand for the blessing, she told herself she had found true love that she had always longed for, and she would never lose it.

Outside the house a Phaeton was waiting for them, and as the Marquis drove away, Neula thought she was leaving an enchanted place.

It was where in the future her mother would be very happy, and which would always, in a way, be her home too.

She put her hand on her husband's knee and said:

"As everything has been done in such a hurry, I have not yet had time to ask where *we* are going."

"Tomorrow, we shall join my yacht at Dover," he answered, "but tonight we are staying half-way there, in a house, very small, but comfortable, which I own."

She looked at him in surprise and he explained:

"It is where I keep some horses, so that they are always ready if I am crossing the Channel, or joining my yacht."

He gave a short laugh before he said:

"I meant to use it for some fair companion who found the distance too exhausting unless we broke the journey."

"Now you . . . are making me . . . jealous!" Neula protested.

"There is no need," the Marquis said. "Actually I have

never stayed there except alone, and all those things are in the past."

He smiled before he added gently:

"You will find I shall settle down and be an exemplary husband. In fact, you may even find me dull!"

His eyes were twinkling as he spoke, and Neula replied:

"You know that is impossible where you are concerned! What I am frightened of is that I shall bore you."

She looked at him wistfully as she continued:

"The gossip says you have been bored hundreds of times, by the beautiful, sophisticated women who laid their hearts and their reputations at your feet!"

"They bored me because they were not you!" the Marquis answered. "I should be very ungrateful if I had not enjoyed the favours they offered me, but what we feel for each other, my darling, is something utterly different."

"H-how can you be . . . sure?"

"I am sure because I have never felt before what you make me feel, and I am going to spend the rest of my life making certain that I never lose the incredible ecstasy I feel when I kiss you."

He spoke so seriously and so movingly that Neula felt the tears come into her eyes.

How could she have imagined that she would ever be so fortunate as to find this handsome, brilliant man?

How could she have imagined that he would love her so completely?

* * *

They reached the Marquis's house which, as he had said, was small, but having been built in Queen Anne's reign was very attractive.

It stood on several acres of ground, and the garden was

brilliant with spring flowers as they drove up to the portioed front-door.

There were far fewer servants that Neula expected, but there was an elderly, experienced housemaid to unpack what she wanted to wear for dinner.

A scented bath was prepared for her in her bedroom which overlooked the garden at the back, with beyond it a vista over the countryside.

The bedroom was decorated in exquisite taste, which she was sure she would find in all the Marquis's houses.

The bed, with its gilded headboard and fresh muslin curtains falling from a gold corola, made her blush.

Then she joined the Marquis downstairs in the Sitting-Room which had comfortable chairs and sofas that she thought only a man would have chosen.

At the same time, the pictures on the wall were a delight, and the crystal chandeliers glistened in the light from many candles.

When she saw the Marquis waiting for her and standing in front of the mantelpiece, she could think only of him.

She ran towards him, wanting his arms and, more than anything else, his lips on hers.

He kissed her until she felt he drew her heart and soul from her body and made it his.

Then he said:

"All the time we have been travelling here, my lovely one, I have been longing to kiss you. I still find it hard to believe that you love me, when I remember how at first I shocked you!"

"How could I have been so foolish?" Neula asked. "But the stories they told me about you were very lurid!"

"I cannot imagine what they will find to talk about in the future!" the Marquis replied, and they both laughed.

They had dinner in the small candlelit Dining-Room,

where the table had been decorated, on the Marquis's instructions, with flowers from the garden.

It was, however, impossible afterwards for Neula to remember what they ate, except that it was delicious and seemed like the ambrosia of the gods.

Only when the meal was over and they had talked for some time after the servants had left the room was Neula aware that there was a touch of fire in the Marquis's eyes when he looked at her.

Finally, finding it difficult to speak, and wanting to be in his arms and to be kissed, she said:

"Perhaps we should . . . go into the . . . other room?"

"As we have had a long and exciting day, my darling," the Marquis replied, "and as tomorrow we shall be leaving fairly early, I have a better idea!"

She knew what he meant without putting it into words.

They went up the staircase together to her room, which adjoined his.

A maid was waiting for her.

When she was undressed and in the beautiful, curtain-draped bed, Neula prayed that she would make the Marquis happy, and not disappoint him.

He came in through a communicating door while she had her eyes closed.

When she opened them he was standing beside the bed.

"Are you praying we shall be happy, my precious?" he asked her.

"Yes . . . and also . . . that I shall not . . . disappoint you."

"It is impossible for you to do that."

He blew out the candle that was burning on his side of the bed, leaving only one burning beside Neula, its light shaded by the muslin curtains.

Then as he got into the bed and drew her close to him, he said:

"You are so beautiful, my adorable wife, but it is so much more than that!"

He turned her face up to his as he spoke and looked down at her. She thought he was about to kiss her, and her lips were ready.

Instead, he kissed her forehead, saying as he did so:

"I love your clever little brain."

Then his lips moved over her arched eyebrows, and touched her eyes before he said:

"I can read what you are thinking in your eyes, and I know we both have an instinct that is stronger than other people's for seeing what is right and wrong. In the future we must together do what is right for all those who follow us."

What he said was so surprising that Neula drew in her breath.

At the same time, her heart within her leapt with the sheer excitement of knowing that this was something he had never said to anybody else.

Just as she knew she had given him her soul, now she possessed his.

Then his lips were on hers.

He was controlling himself to be very gentle because she was so young and, as he knew, pure and untouched.

He kissed her lips, the softness of her neck, and each of her breasts, until he felt her moving closer to him.

He knew he had aroused a little flame within her in response to the fire that was consuming him.

"I love you, my darling," he said hoarsely, "and I want you! God knows, I want you, but I am afraid of frightening or shocking you."

"You could . . . never do . . . that!" Neula whispered. "When you . . . kiss me as you are . . . doing now . . . I feel that you are . . . carrying me into the . . . sky."

She smiled at him as she continued:

"Our love is . . . part of God . . . and so perfect that the . . . angels are . . . singing."

The way she spoke made the Marquis's kisses become more demanding, more possessive.

She found that love was not the soft, gentle thing she had always believed it to be.

Instead, it was fierce, strong, irresistible; a power and a force, and no one could withstand it.

Then, as she felt the flames he had ignited in her flickering through her whole body, she knew she would never have been able to hide from him for long.

The love they felt for each other was stronger than any convention or fear which had made her feel she must go away.

Love was irresistible.

The love she had for the Marquis made her his captive, and she could never escape from him, however long she might live.

"I love . . . you!" she heard herself saying not only with her lips, but with her whole body as his heart beat against hers.

"I adore you! I worship you!" the Marquis replied. "You are mine—mine for all eternity! My precious—give me yourself!"

"I am . . . yours . . . all yours!"

Then, as they passed through the gates of Paradise into a Heaven of their own, the angels were singing, and the power that swept through them was Divine.

*   *   *

Six days later the Marquis walked into the Drawing-Room, where Neula was waiting for him.

161

She gave a cry of delight as he appeared and ran towards him.

He put his arms round her and held her close.

He kissed her, and it was a long, very passionate kiss, before he asked:

"Have you missed me?"

"I feel I have been . . . alone for a . . . century!"

He laughed.

"It was actually only four hours, but I have brought you back the newspapers from Falmouth. They are somewhat out of date, but there is a description of Sir Horace's Funeral which I think might interest you."

The Marquis held out a copy of *The Times* and she took it from him reluctantly and spread it out on a table.

As she bent over it, she felt his lips on her hair, then on her bare neck.

"If you do . . . that," she murmured, "I shall not be able to . . . read about that . . . horrible man!"

"He will trouble you no more," the Marquis said. "What I really wanted you to see was a reference to your mother."

Nervously Neula looked to where, following a formal report of Sir Horace's Funeral, was a list of the people who were present.

She read:

Lady Harlow was unfortunately absent owing to ill-health. It is understood that she is convalescing abroad, and will not be returning to England for some time.

Neula gave a sigh of relief.

"If everybody believes that, there will be no scandal!"

"That is what I thought," the Marquis said. "I can only commend whichever one of his relatives it was who thought of anything so intelligent to explain your mother's absence."

"At least no one will . . . think it . . . at all strange."

"I agree and that is what matters," the Marquis said.

Neula pushed the newspaper aside and put her arms round his neck.

"Did you think of me while you were away?"

"You are fishing for compliments," he answered. "I thought about you all the way there."

He smiled down at her and went on:

"I pushed my horses in a most reprehensible manner on the way home because I was so eager to be with you again!"

"Oh, darling, that is what I hoped you would feel! But were the horses you went to see worth the journey?"

"I bought four," the Marquis replied. "They are coming here tomorrow, and you can tell me then what you think of them."

"I am sure, if you chose them, they will be marvellous," Neula said, "and I am longing to be able to ride with you again."

They were in what Neula thought was one of the loveliest houses she had ever seen, with its garden extending to the very edge of the cliffs.

Yet she had not realised at first that the stables were empty.

But the Marquis had wanted to ride, and heard that there were some excellent horses in a sale at Falmouth.

He therefore had set off four days after they had arrived and she knew that any horses he purchased would be the very best obtainable.

Now she said softly:

"It will be very exciting to ride with you, but I hope we do not find any Russian Princes lurking in the woods!"

"I am sure there will be only the Cornish Piskies in which I am sure you believe," the Marquis smiled. "They will give us good warning, and, of course, as you are with me, I shall be fully protected."

"I suppose, because I love you so much," Neula said, "I am always afraid that something dreadful may happen!"

She paused a moment and then went on:

"For instance, I am afraid that this all may be only a dream, and I shall wake up to find you do not really exist."

The Marquis laughed and pulled her a little closer.

"I will prove it to you so that there will be no mistake, that I do exist!" he said. "In fact, as I have had a long journey, I intend now to have a bath and a rest before dinner."

He saw the light in Neula's eyes and added:

"That is the polite word for it, but the French call it '*cinq-à-sept*'!"

"The girls in Florence used to talk about it," Neula said, "but I was never certain what they meant."

"Then it is something I will be delighted to explain," the Marquis replied.

He kissed her, then quickly, as if he were afraid that she would delay him, went off to have his bath.

As he left the room Neula picked up *The Times*, folded it, and put it away in a corner, hoping the Marquis would not refer to it again.

She longed to forget the way Sir Horace had treated her mother and she felt sure that was what she also was trying to do.

They had one very happy letter from Louise, which had been forwarded on from Tremaine Park.

She wrote:

We are very happy, Dearest, as I know you will be happy with Drogo. He is everything Papa and I

*would have wanted you to find in a husband, but I
never imagined, as we had no money, that you would
be lucky enough to meet anybody not only so attractive but so important. . . .*

"It does seem like a fairy-story," Neula said to herself as
she went upstairs to her bedroom.

There was no maid to help her undress, which was what
she preferred.

She wanted only to be alone with the Marquis, and too
many servants were inclined to get in the way.

Tomkins was different. He would disappear as soon as
he knew he was not wanted.

Neula thought he looked on them as two children whom
he had to look after, while at the same time making sure
that they enjoyed themselves.

The windows looked out over the garden towards the
sea which was shimmering in the rays of the sun that was
gradually sinking over the horizon.

'It is so wonderful!' Neula thought. 'I wish we might
never have to leave it, but could stay here forever!'

But she knew there were many calls on the Marquis in
looking after all the people on his estates.

She was sure, too, that his voice was urgently needed in
the House of Lords to speak on the Reform Bill.

"I must inspire and help him to do what is right," she
told herself.

Then as the door opened and he came into the room, it
was impossible to think of anything but how handsome he
was and how much she loved him.

She knew, as he drew her to him as if he were a magnet,
that since he felt the same about her, theirs was a perfect,
inexpressible union of mind, heart, and spirit.

The Marquis lifted her up in his arms and carried her to the bed.

He laid her down against the pillows, and sat down beside her.

Taking her hand in his, he said:

"I keep asking myself how is it possible for you to be lovelier every time I see you."

"And I ask myself how is it . . . possible to . . . love you more . . . every day than I did the day . . . before!"

The Marquis kissed her hand.

Then as he got into bed she knew that later tonight she would find, although it seemed impossible, that she loved him, even more than she loved him at this moment.

He felt her body move against his.

"I love you."

"I . . . love . . . you!"

They were words they had spoken a thousand times but which always thrilled her.

Then his lips held her captive and once again they were flying towards their special Heaven, where the angels were singing.

ABOUT THE AUTHOR

Barbara Cartland, the world's most famous romantic novelist, who is also an historian, playwright, lecturer, political speaker and television personality, has now written over 450 books and sold over 450 million books the world over.

She has also had many historical works published and has written four autobiographies as well as the biographies of her mother and that of her brother, Ronald Cartland, who was the first Member of Parliament to be killed in the last war. This book has a preface by Sir Winston Churchill and has just been republished with an introduction by Sir Arthur Bryant.

Love at the Helm, a novel written with the help and inspiration of the late Admiral of the Fleet, the Earl Mountbatten of Burma, is being sold for the Mountbatten Memorial Trust.

Miss Cartland in 1978 sang an Album of Love Songs with the Royal Philharmonic Orchestra.

In 1976 by writing twenty-one books, she broke the world record and has continued for the following nine years with twenty-four, twenty, twenty-three, twenty-four, twenty-four, twenty-five, twenty-three, twenty-six, and twenty-two. She is in the *Guinness Book of Records* as the best-selling author in the world.

She is unique in that she was one and two in the Dalton List of Best Sellers, and one week had four books in the top twenty.

In private life Barbara Cartland, who is a Dame of the Order of St. John of Jerusalem, Chairman of the St. John Council in Hertfordshire and Deputy President of the St. John Ambulance Brigade, has also fought for better conditions and salaries for Midwives and Nurses.

Barbara Cartland is deeply interested in Vitamin Therapy and is President of the British National Association for Health. Her book *The Magic of Honey* has sold throughout the world and is translated into many languages. Her designs "Decorating with Love" are being sold all over the U.S.A., and the National Home Fashions League named her in 1981, "Woman of Achievement."

In 1984 she received at Kennedy Airport America's Bishop Wright Air Industry Award for her contribution to the development of aviation; in 1931 she and two R.A.F. Officers thought of, and carried, the first aeroplane-towed glider air-mail.

Barbara Cartland's Romances (a book of cartoons) has been published in Great Britain and the U.S.A., as well as a cookery book, *The Romance of Food*, and *Getting Older, Growing Younger*. She has recently written a children's pop-up picture book, entitled *Princess to the Rescue*.